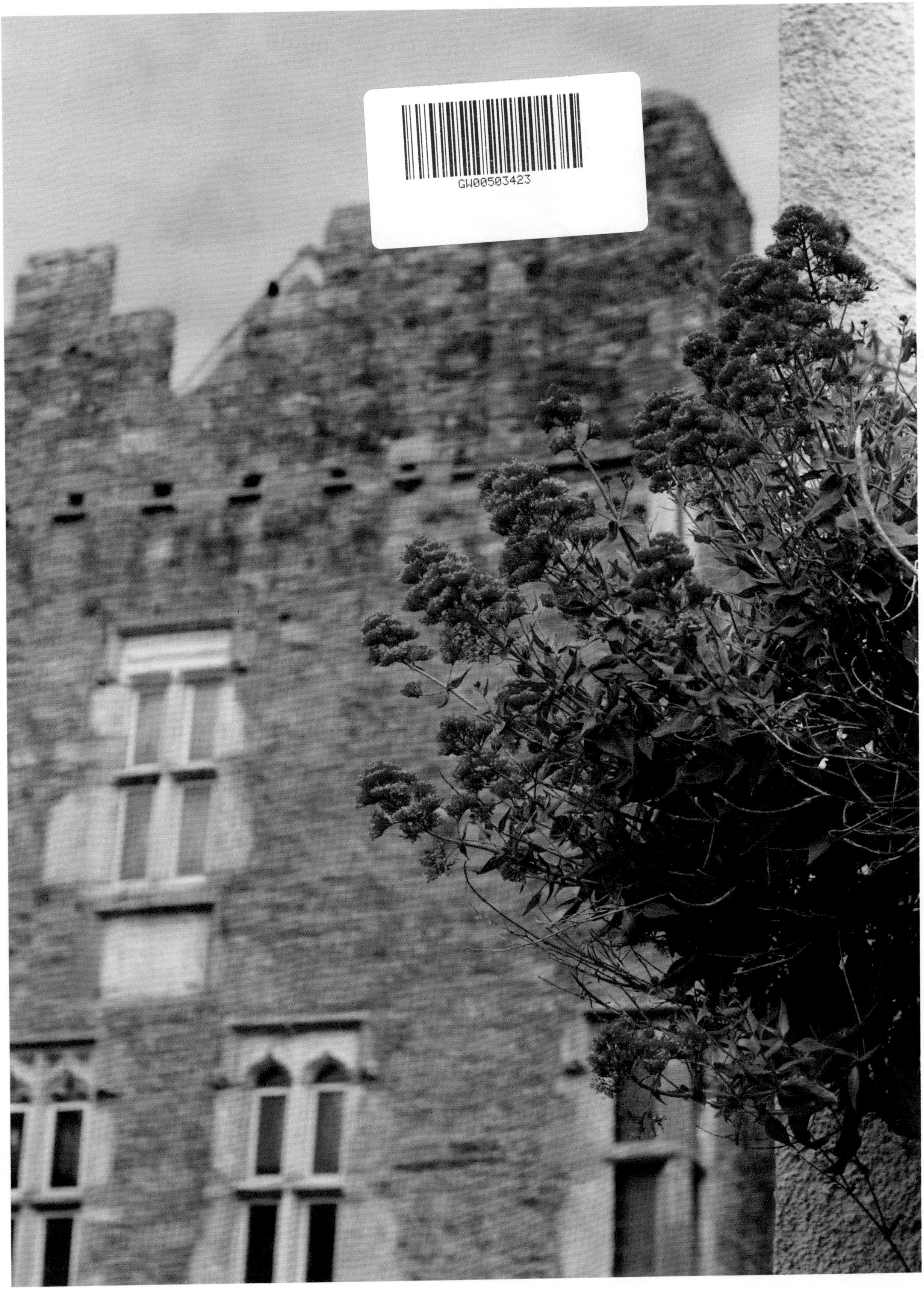

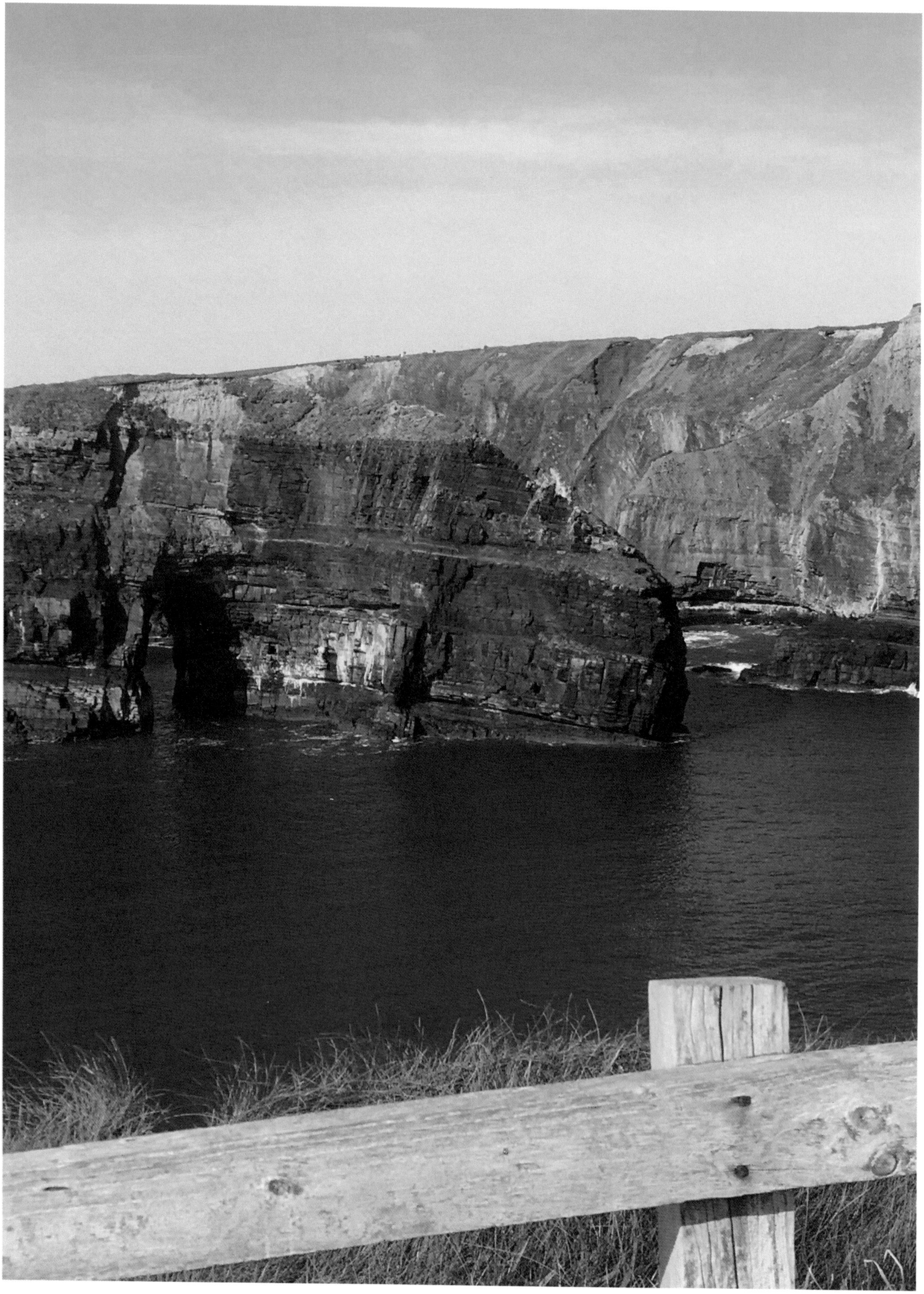

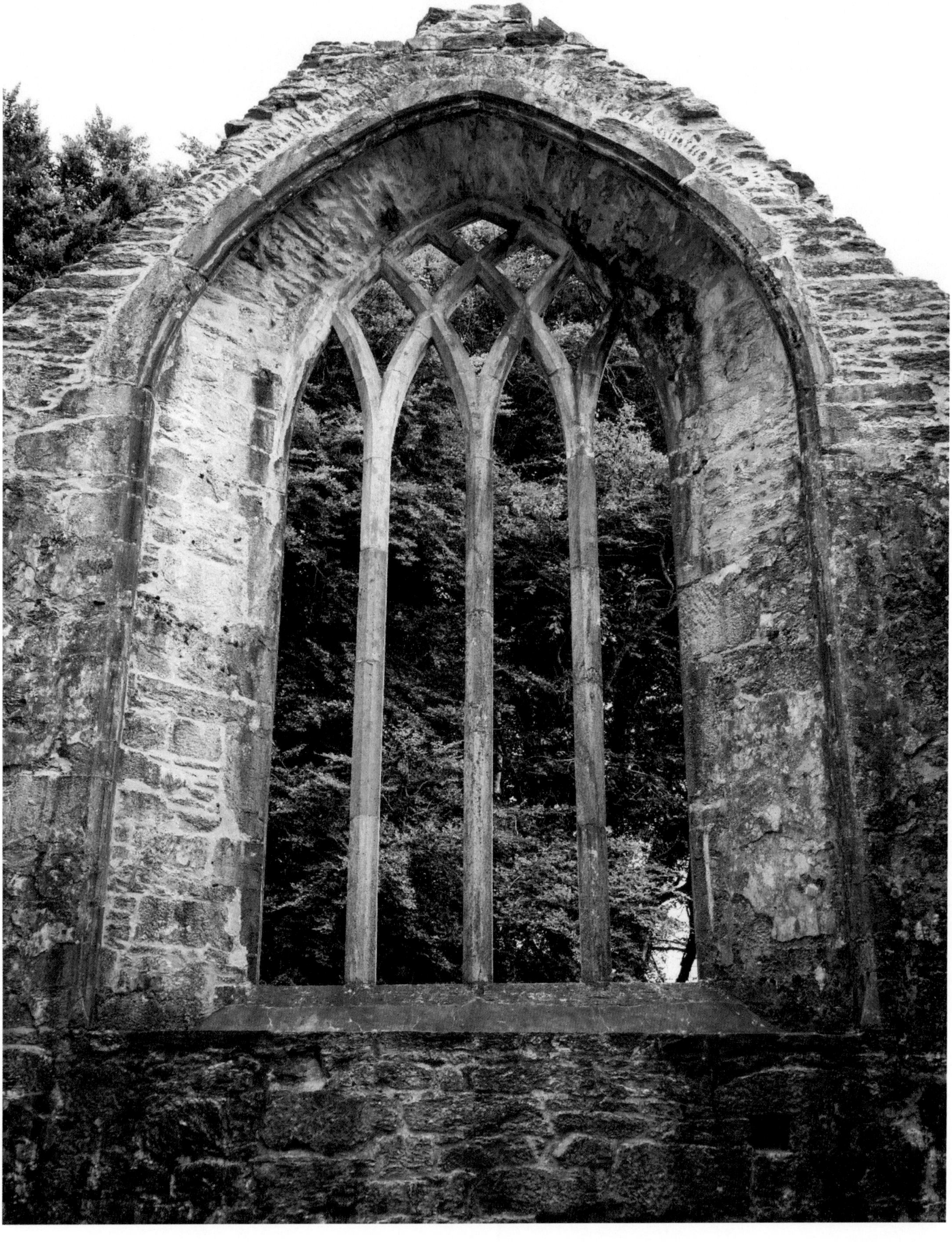

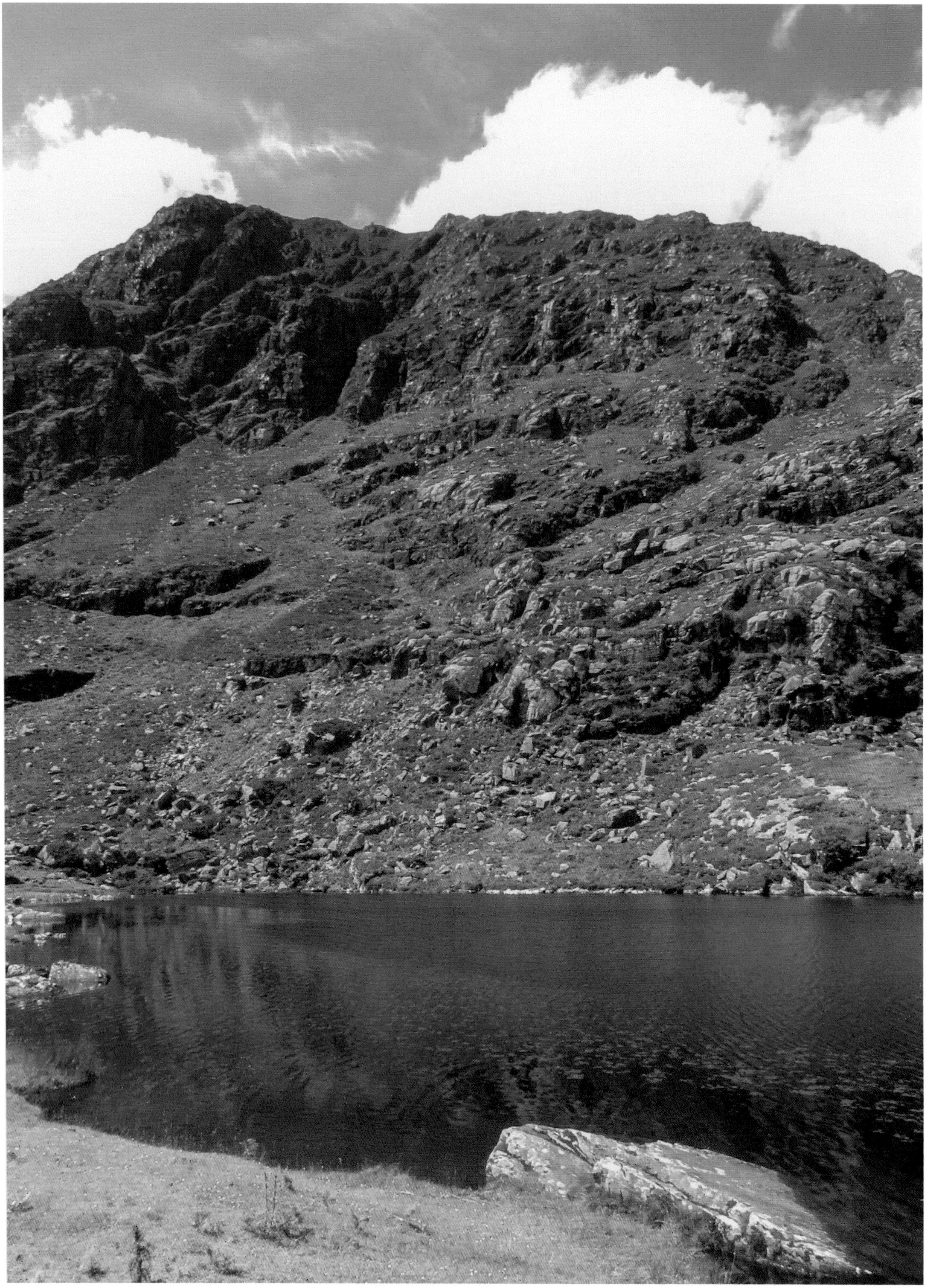

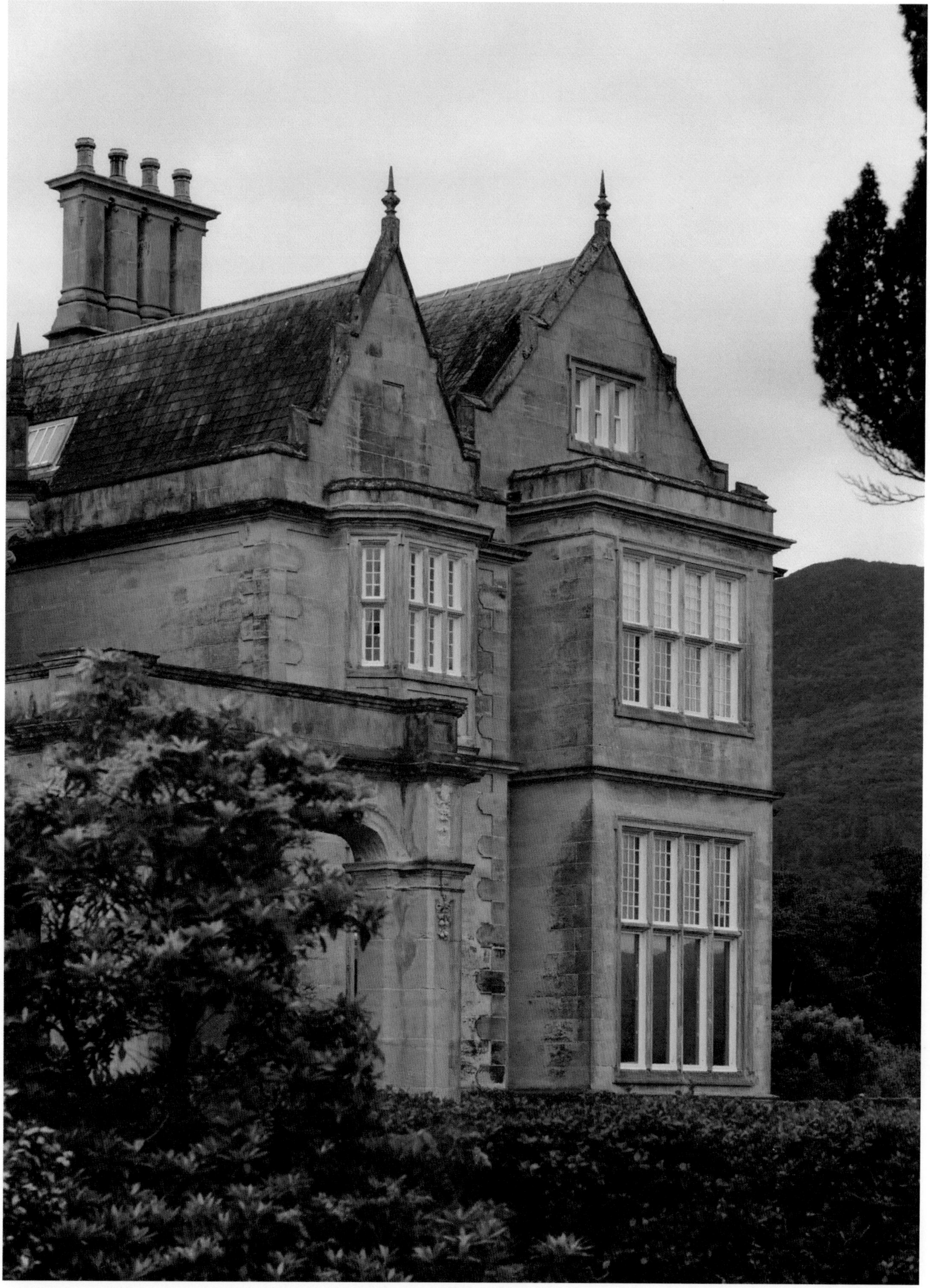

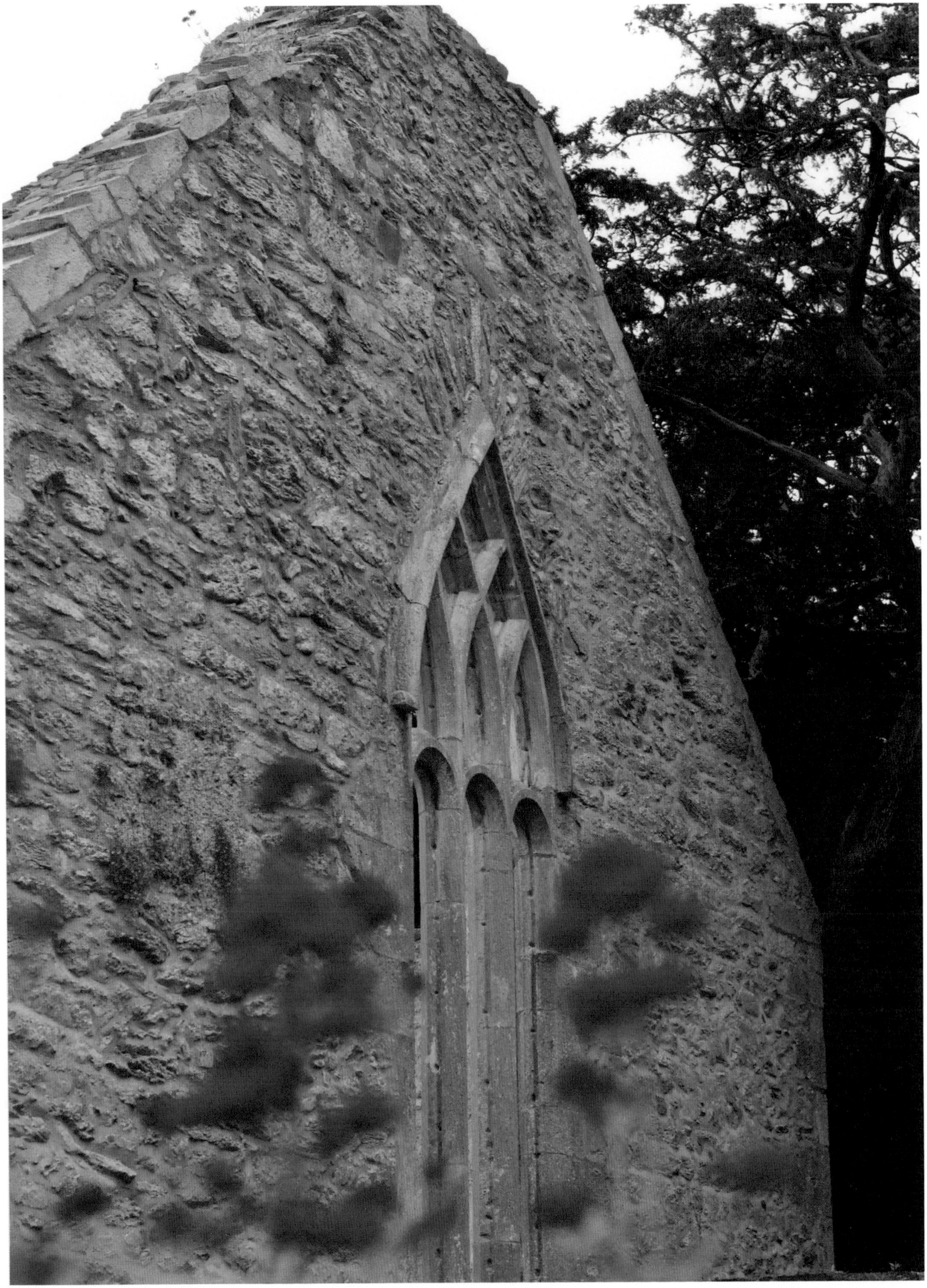

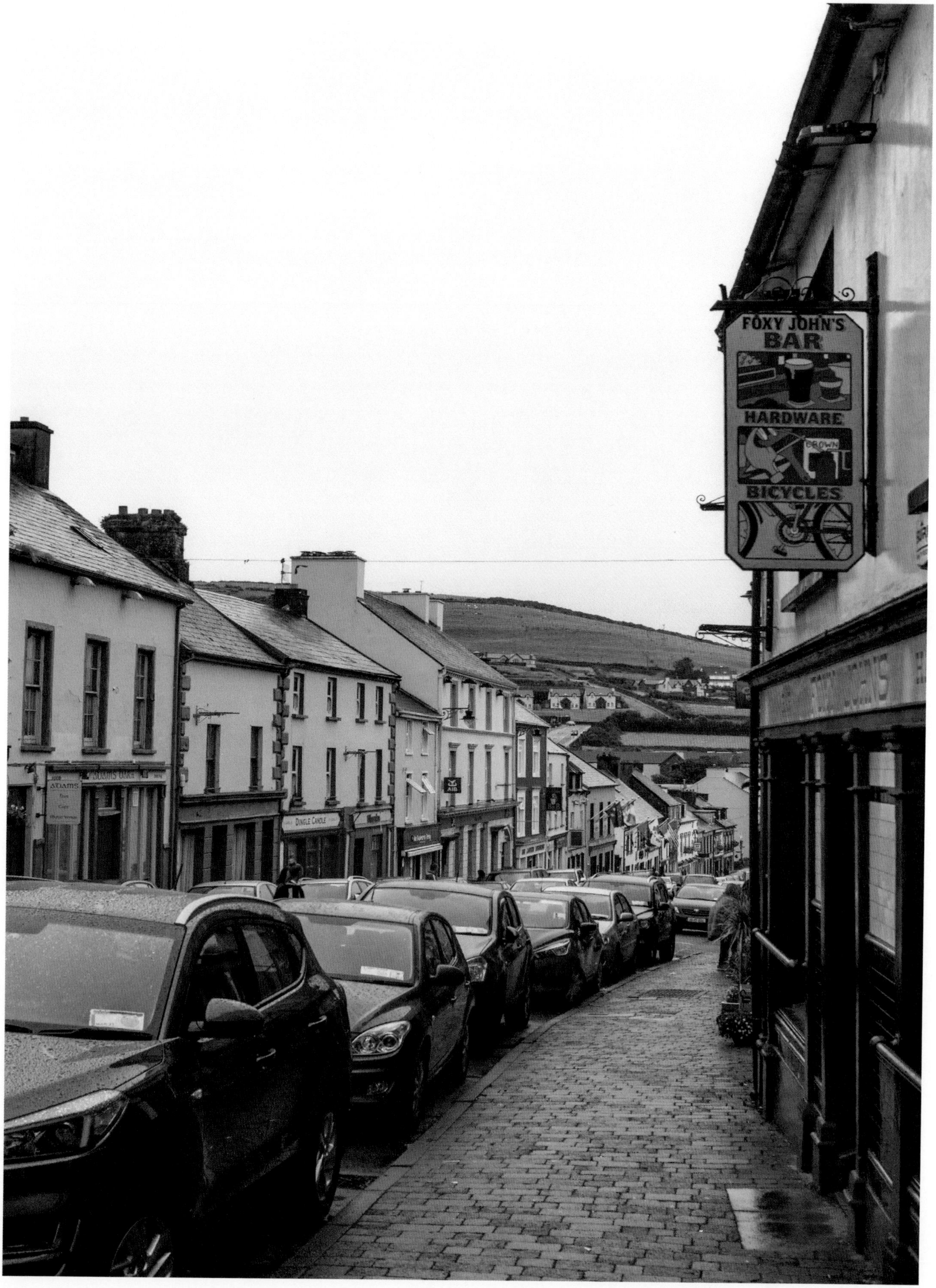
FOXY JOHN'S
BAR
HARDWARE
BICYCLES
DINGLE CANDLE
AIB

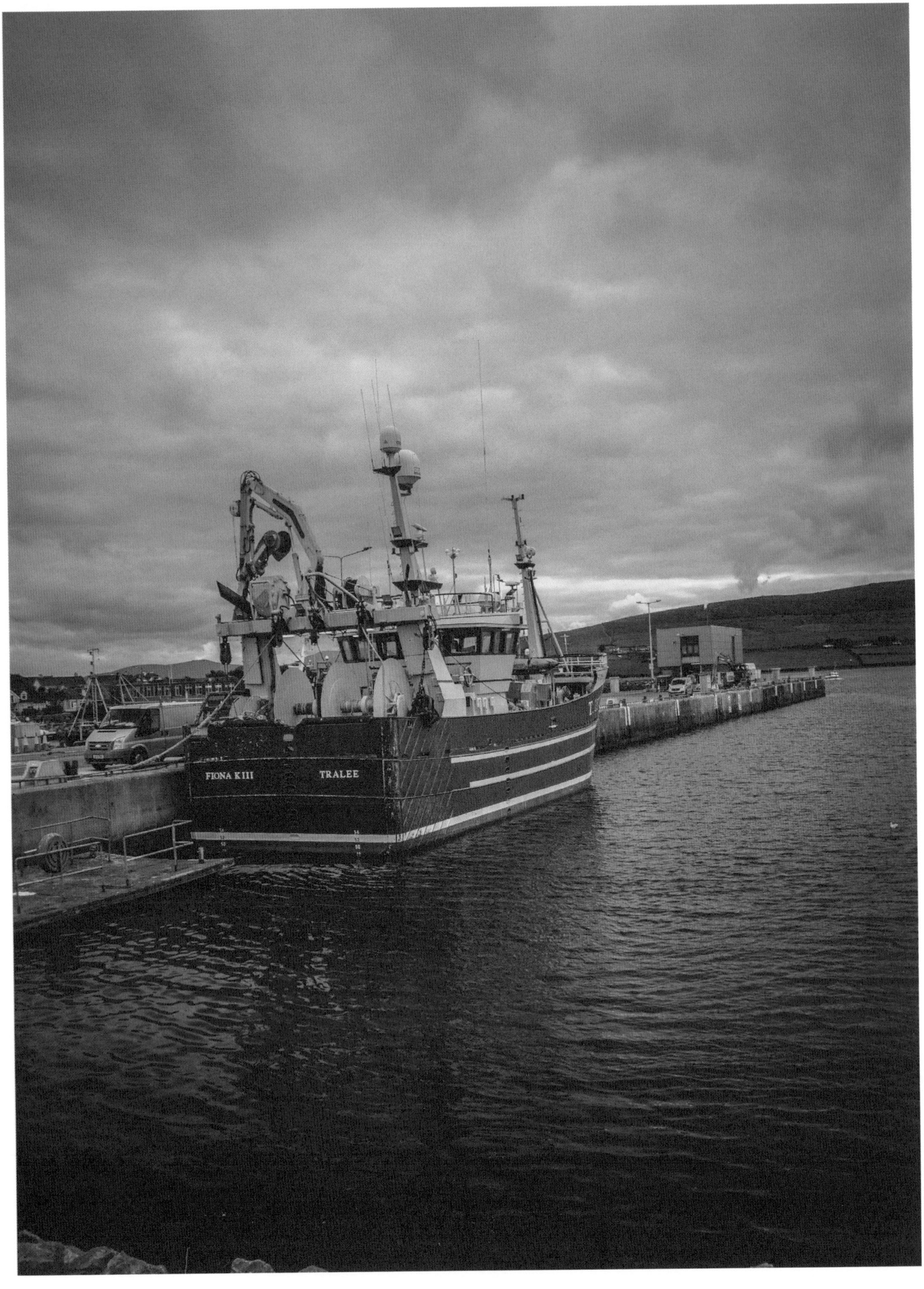
FIONA K III
TRALEE

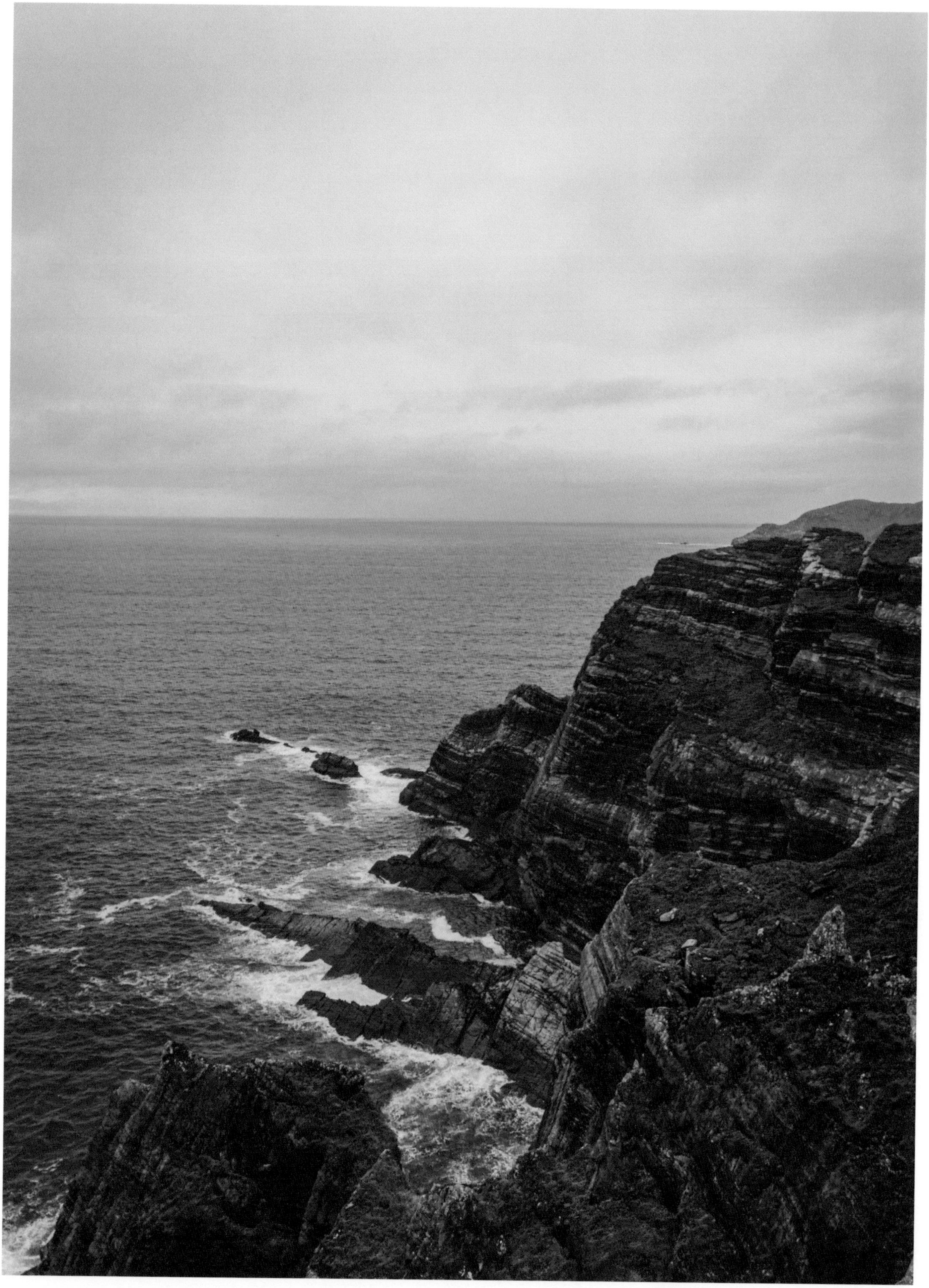

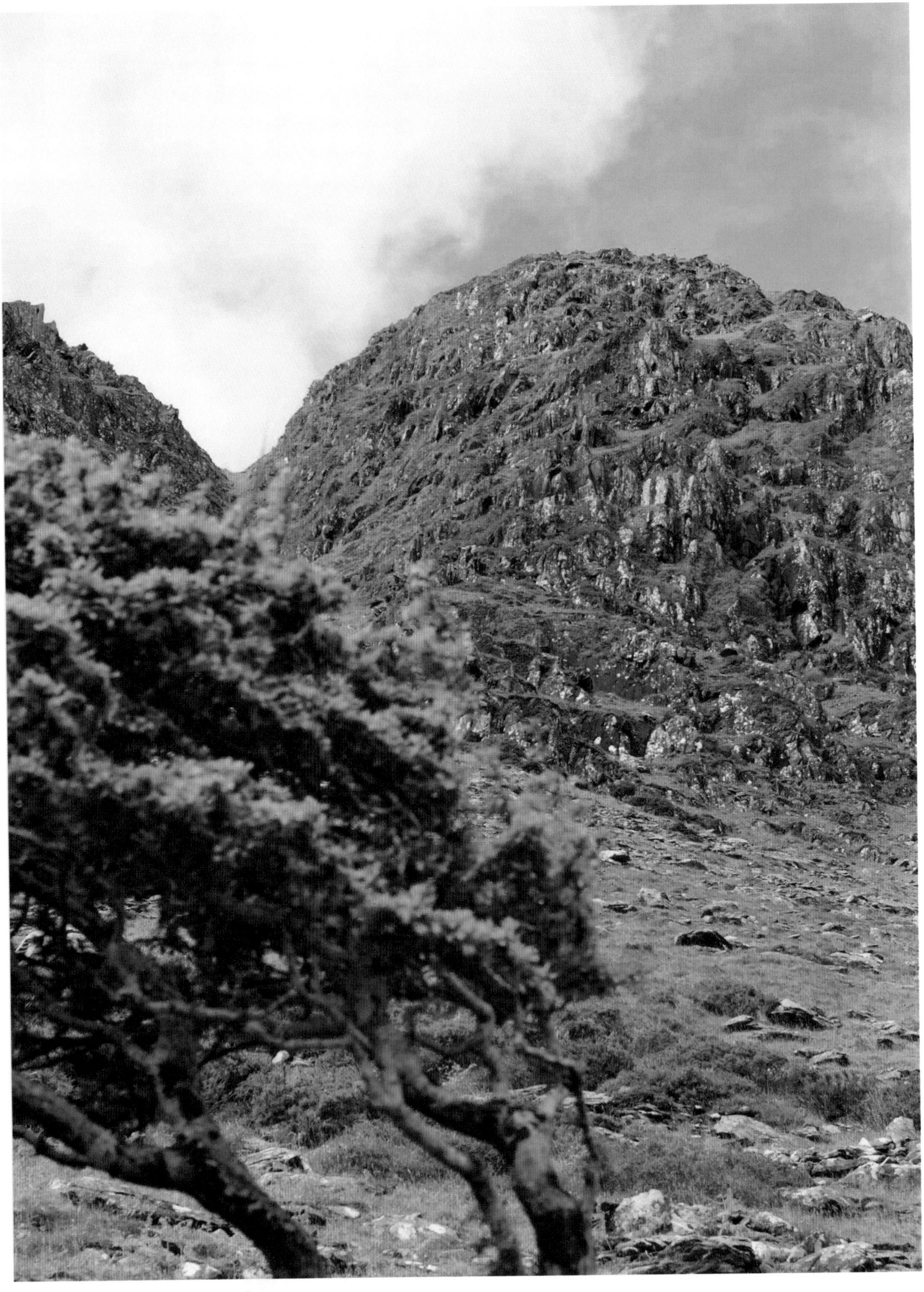

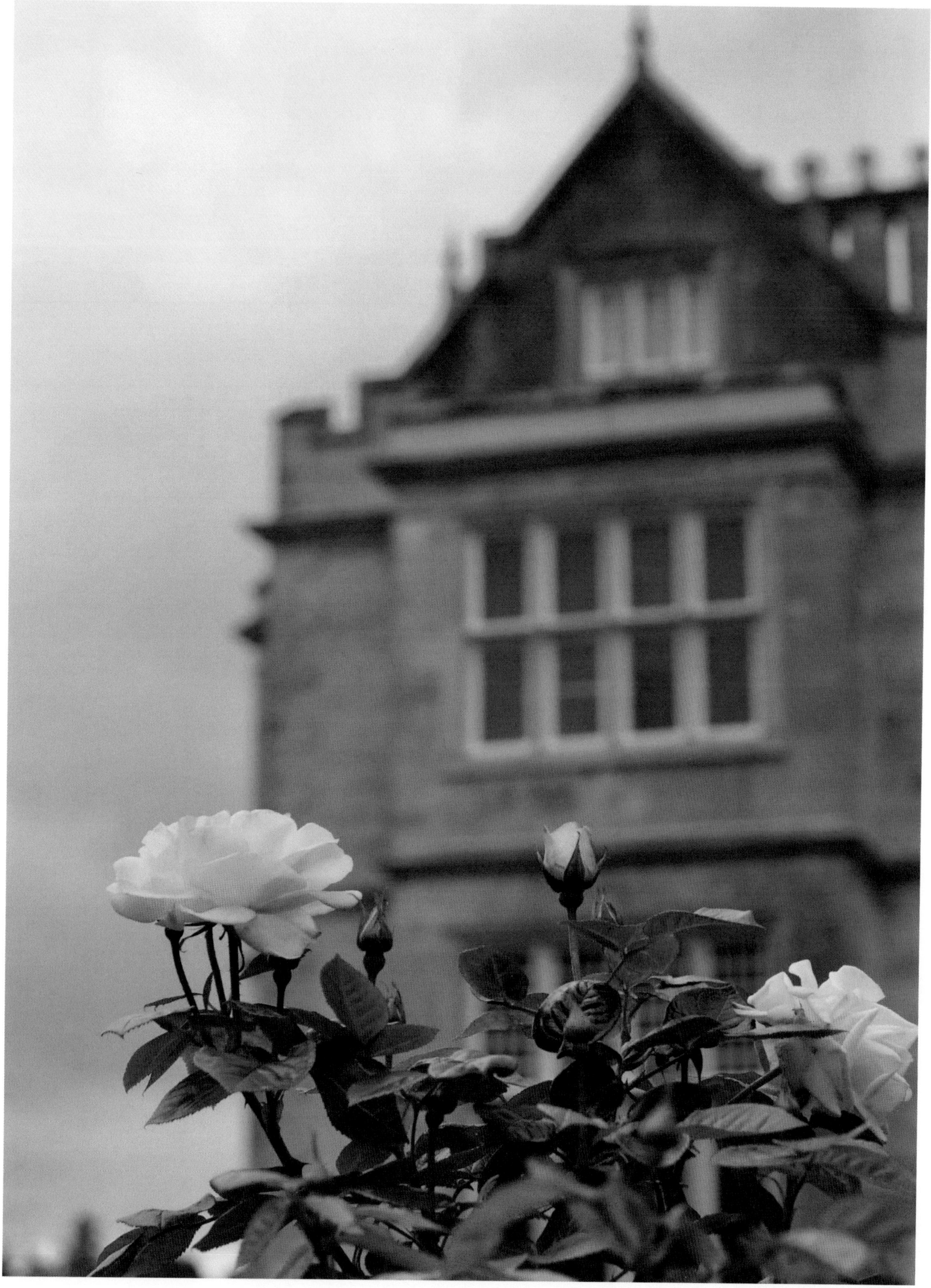

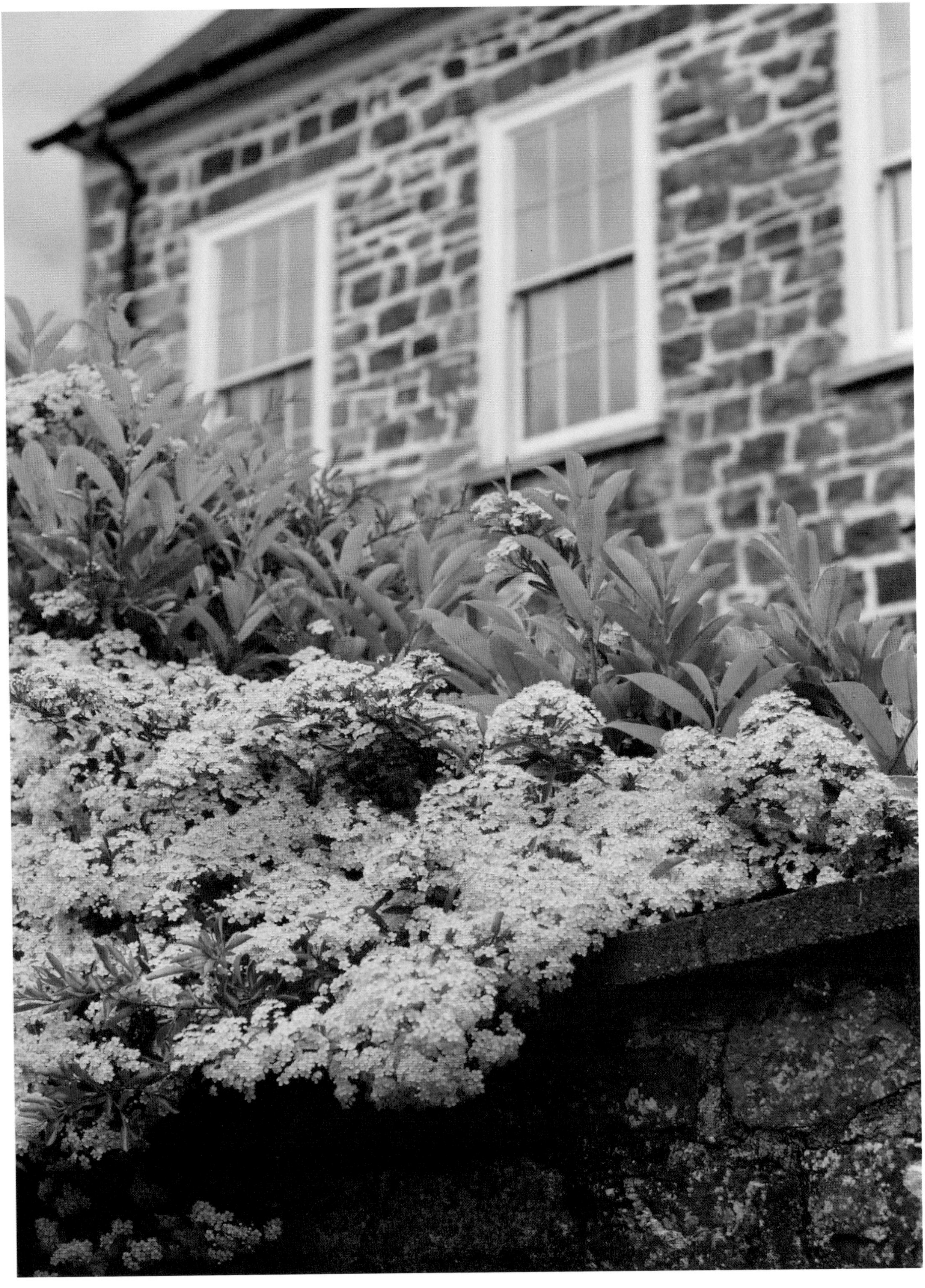

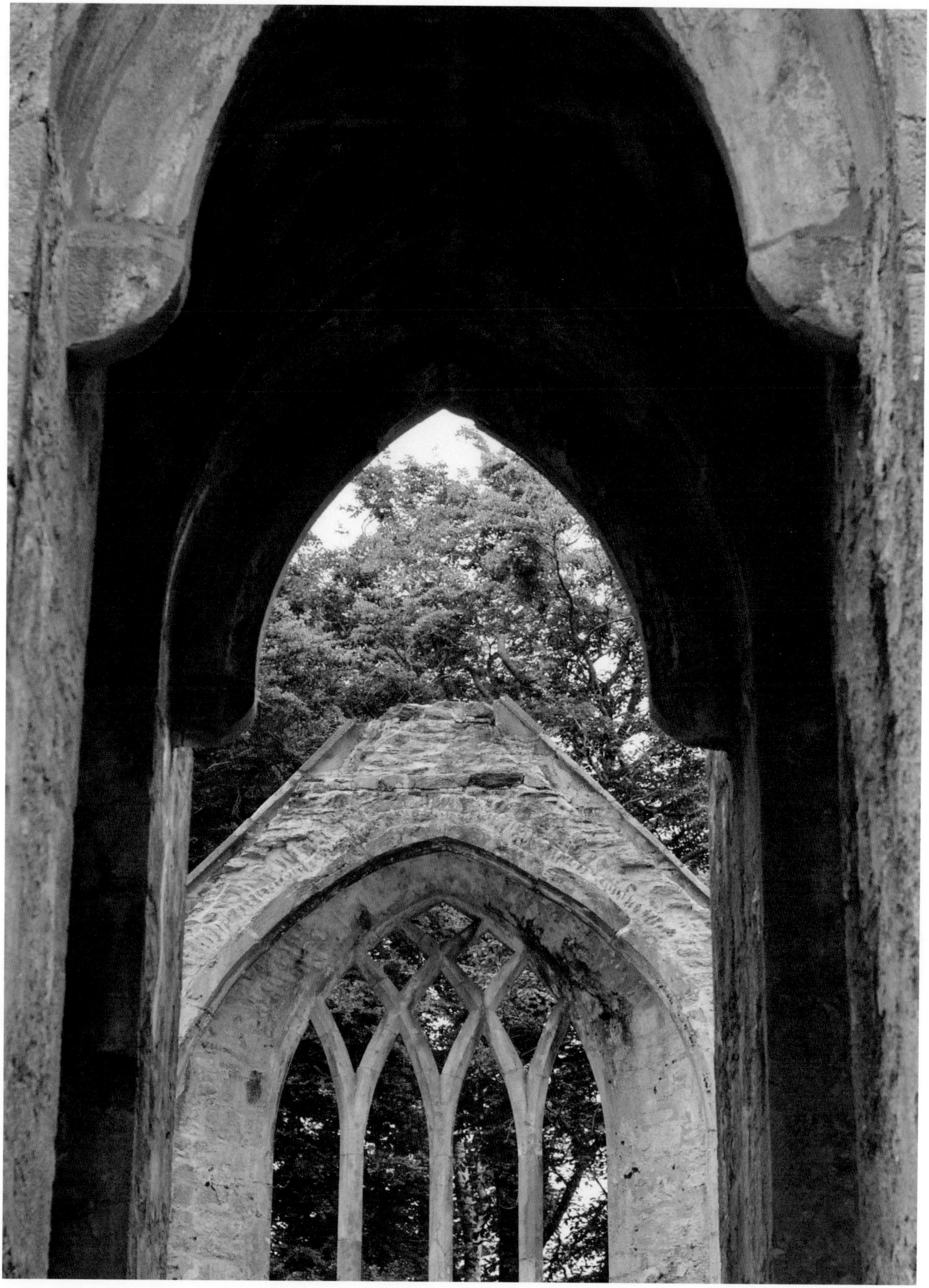

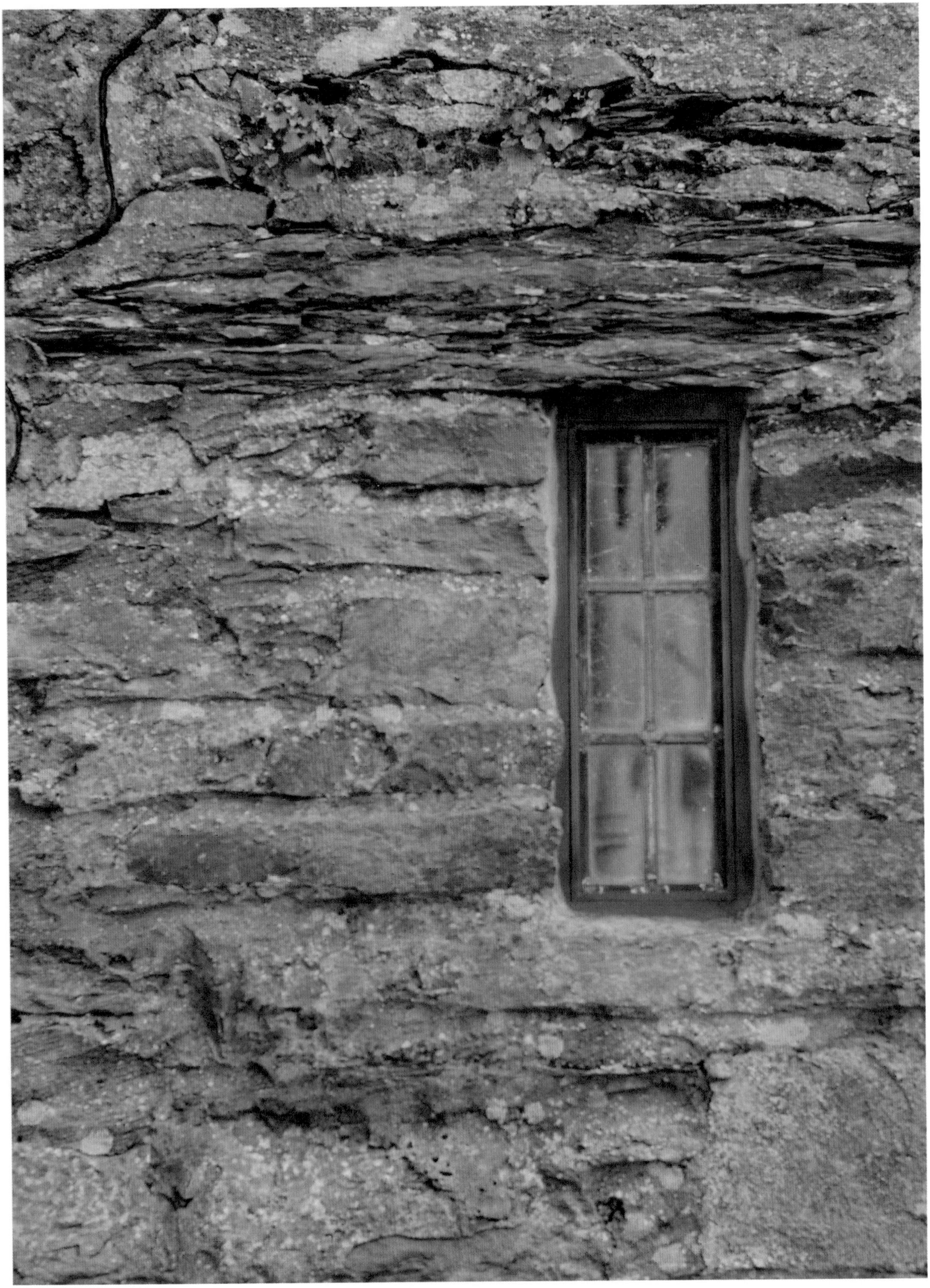

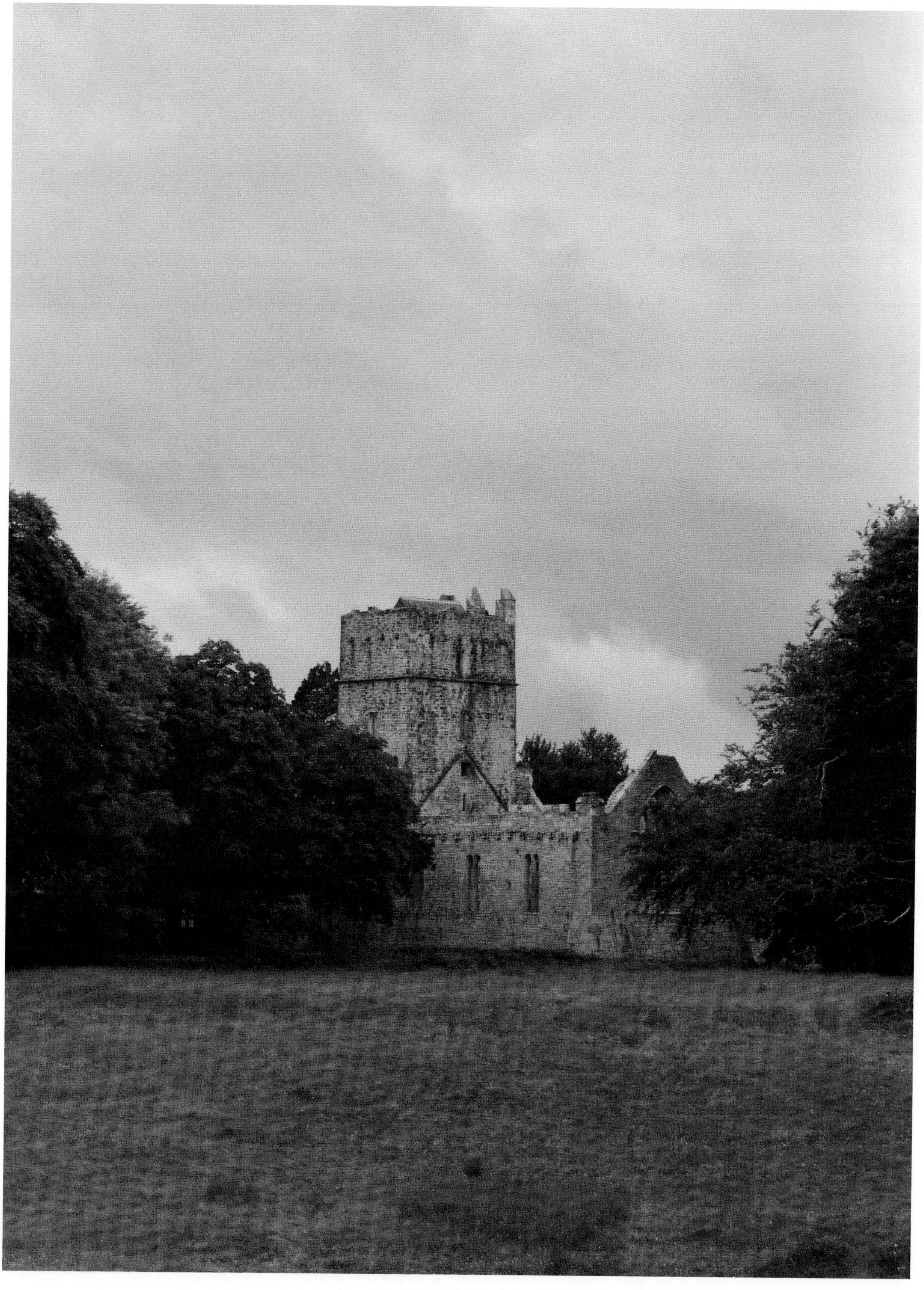

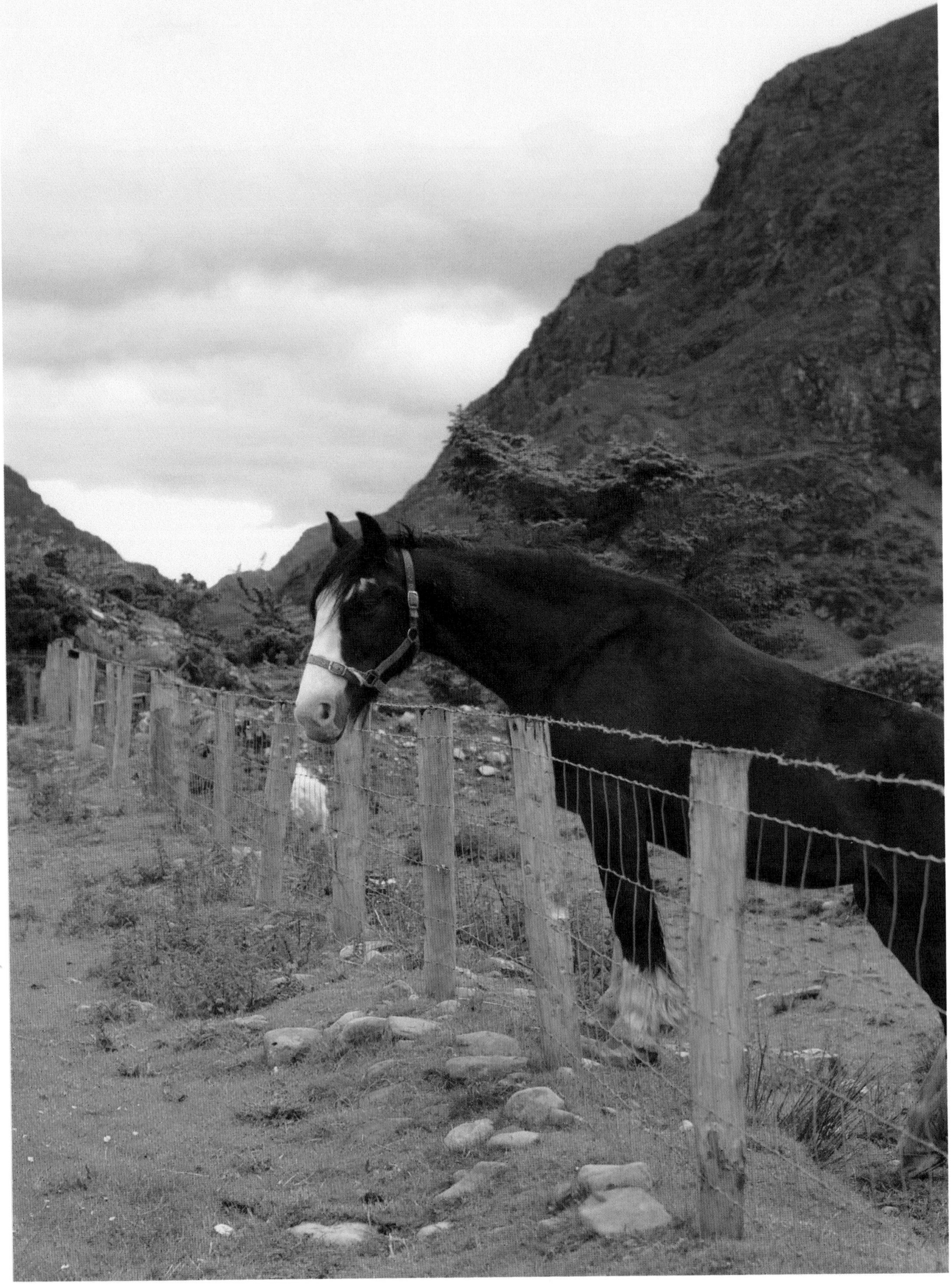

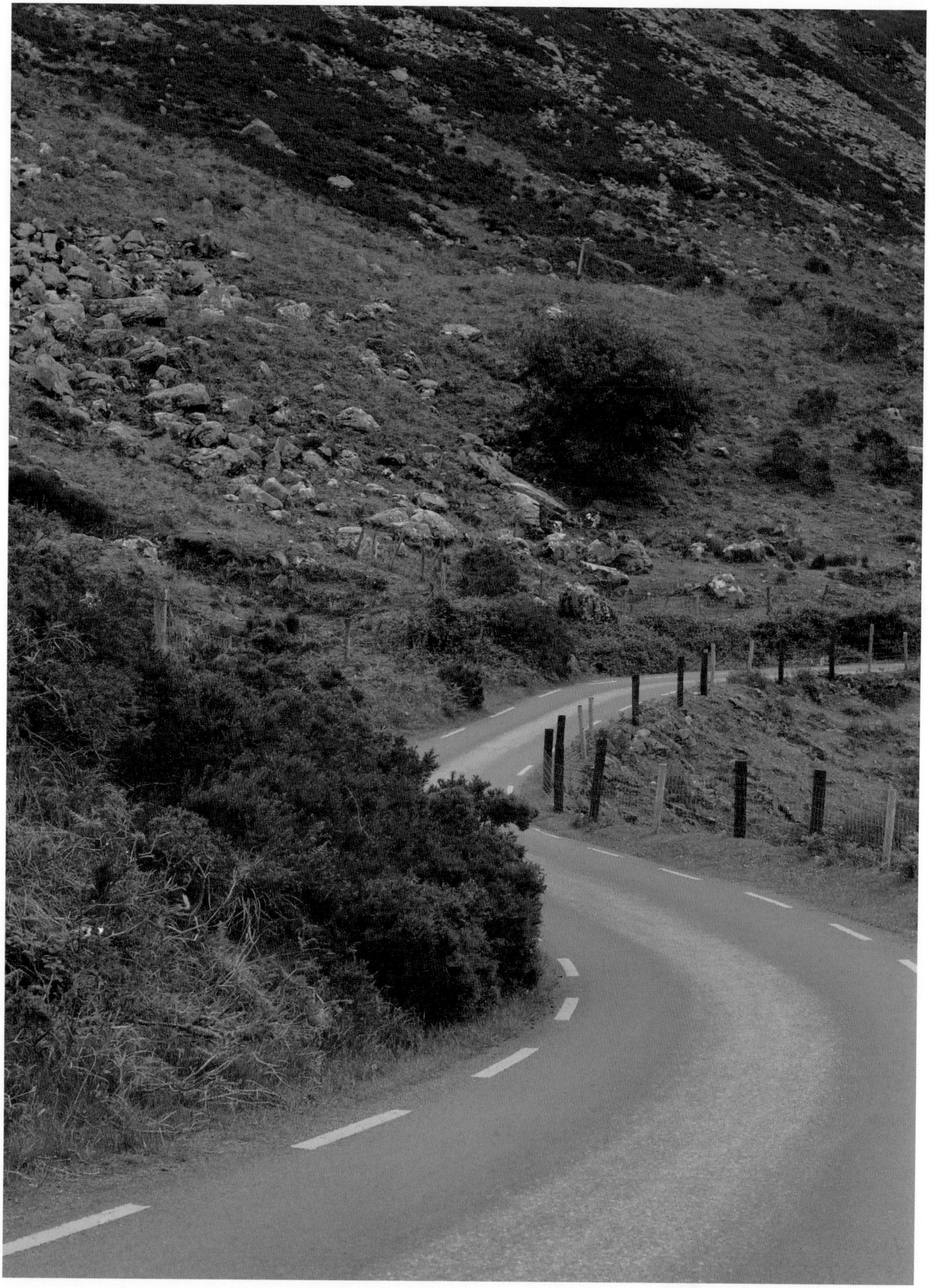

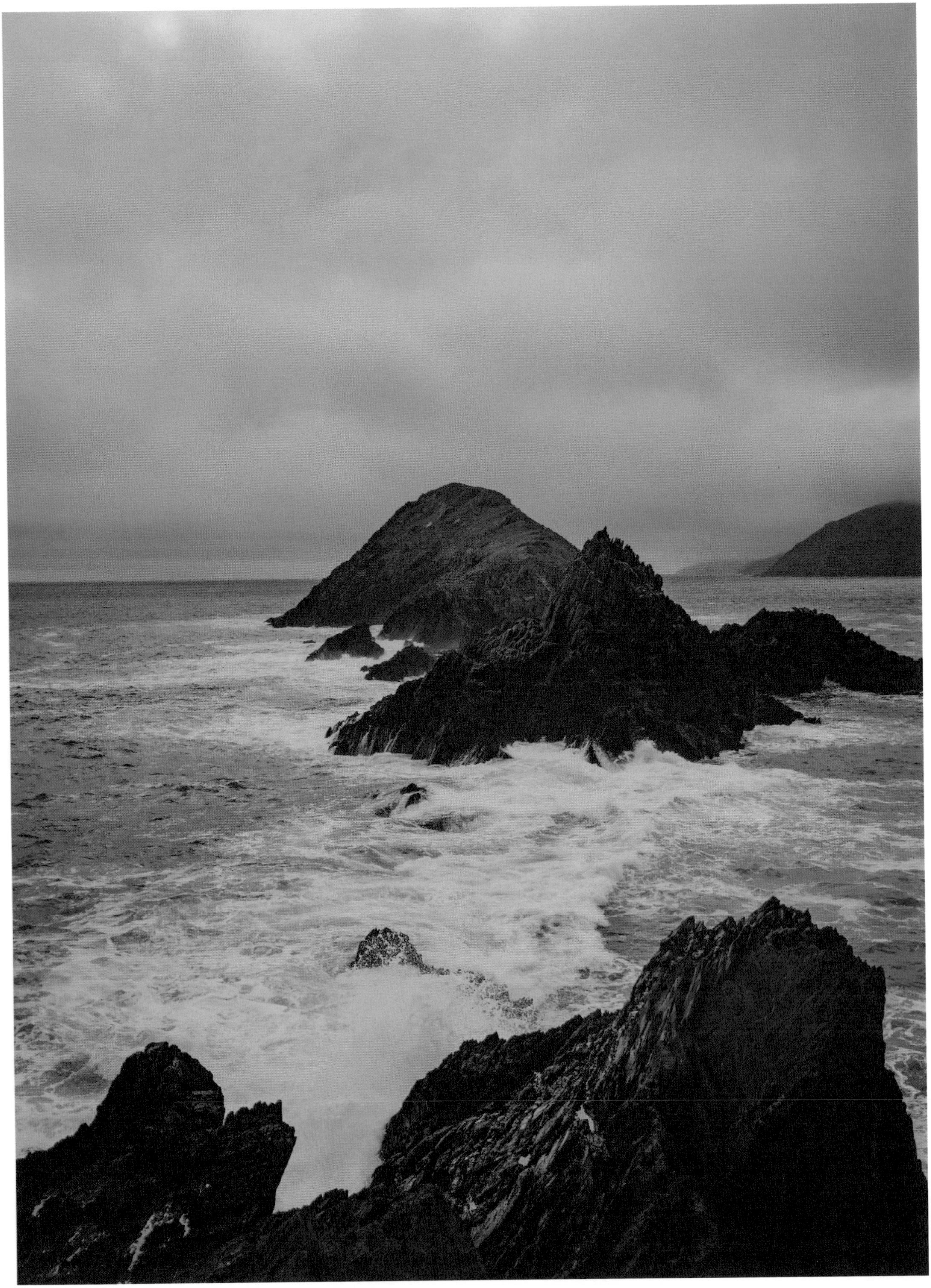

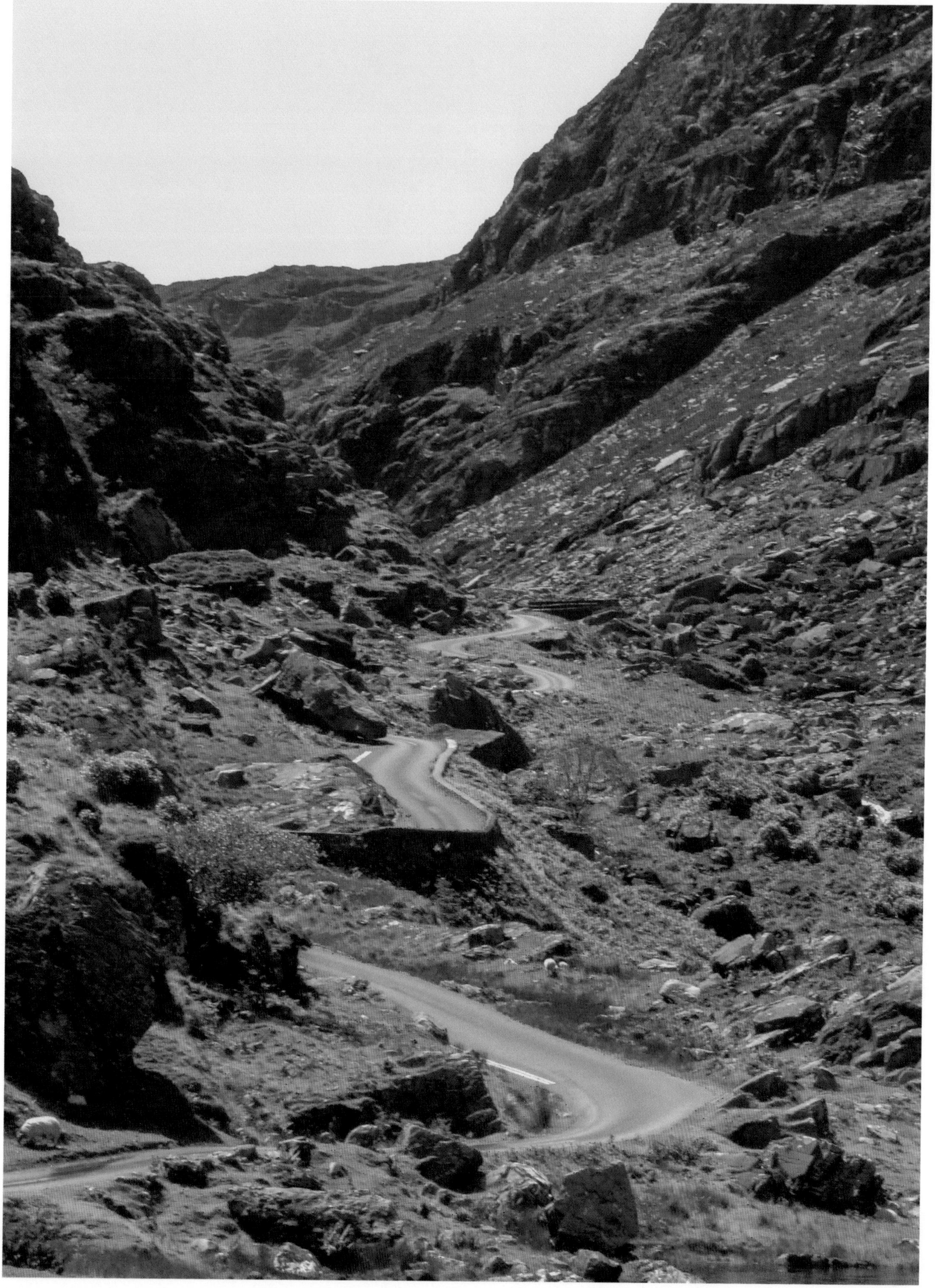

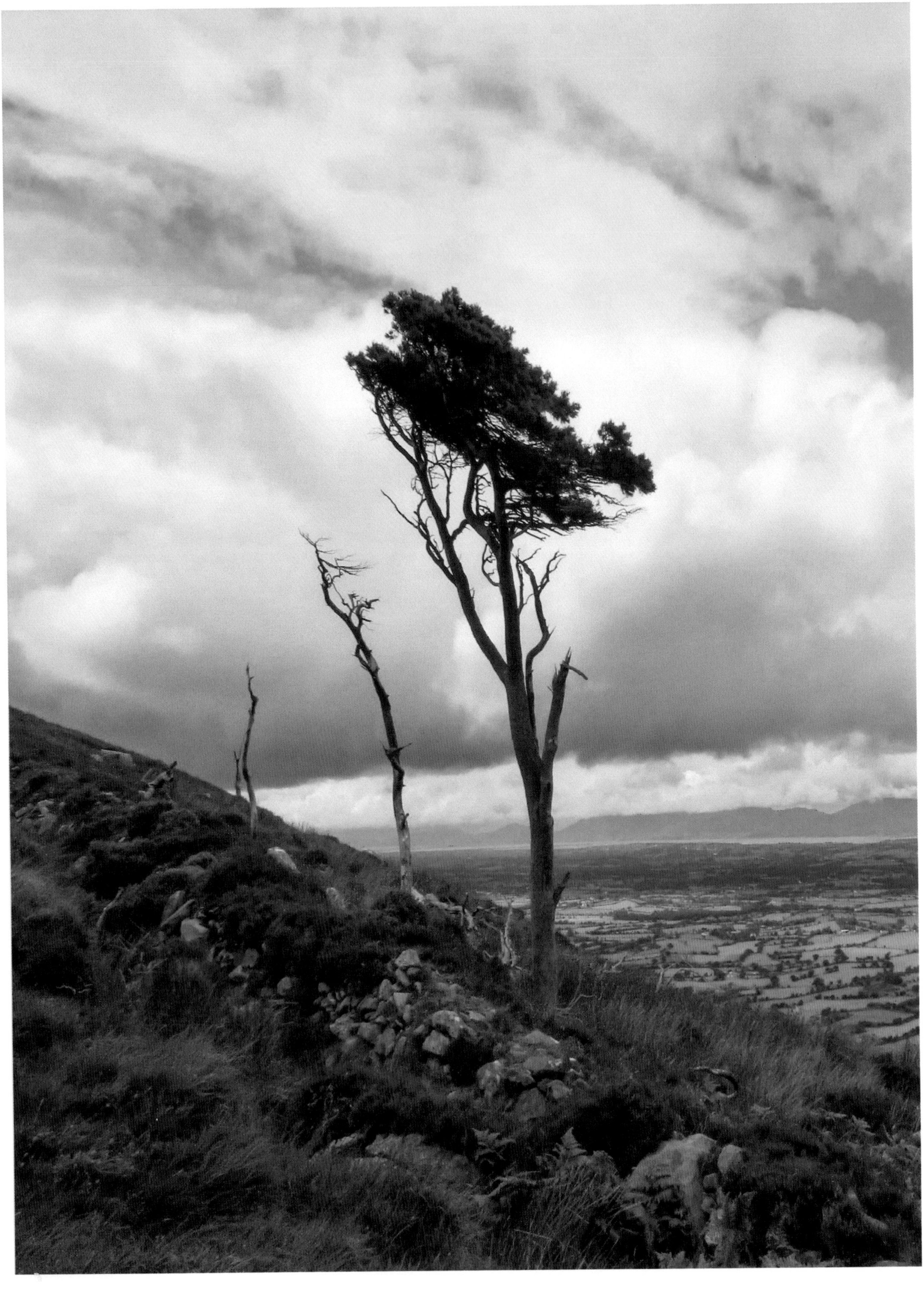

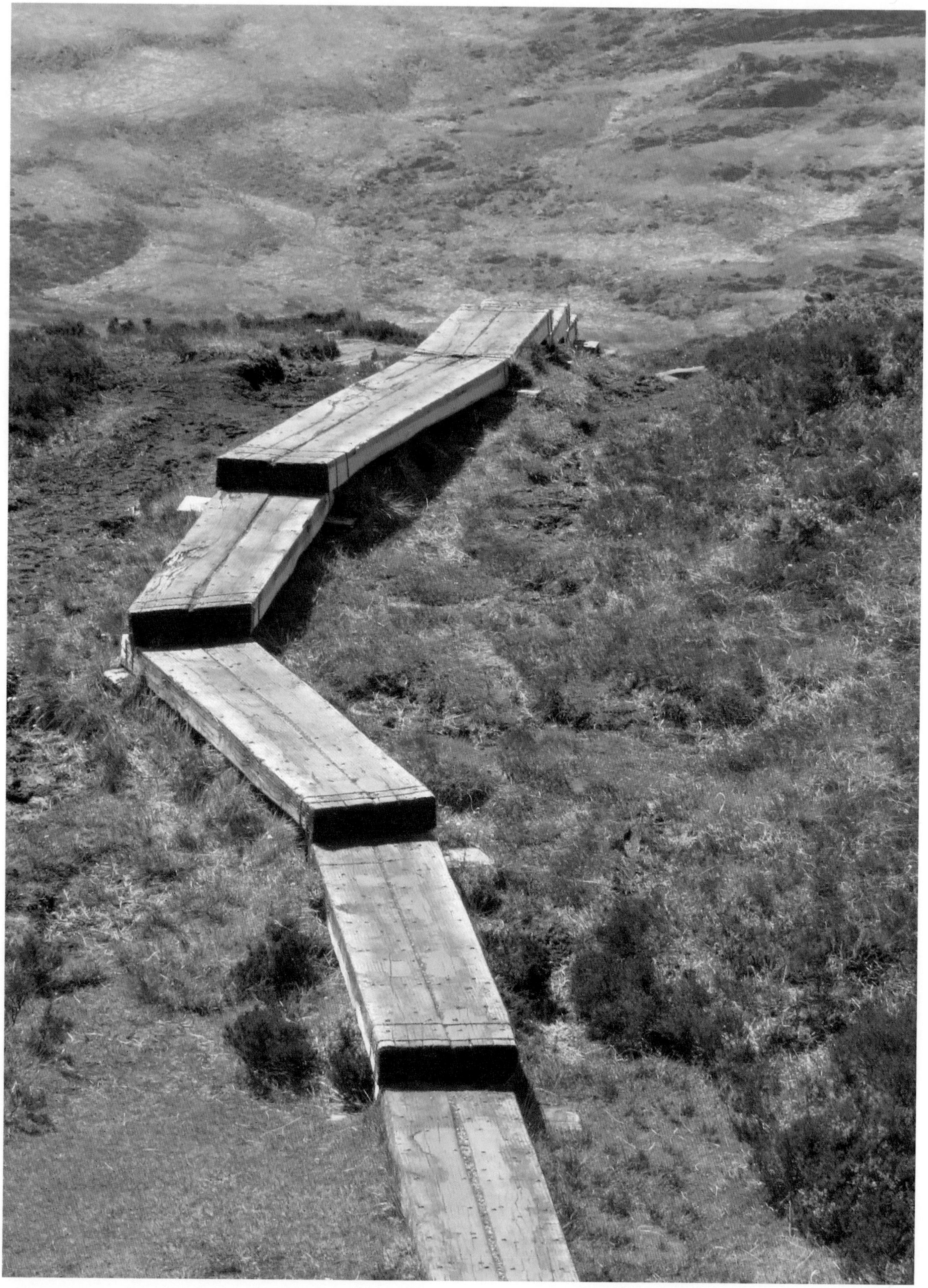

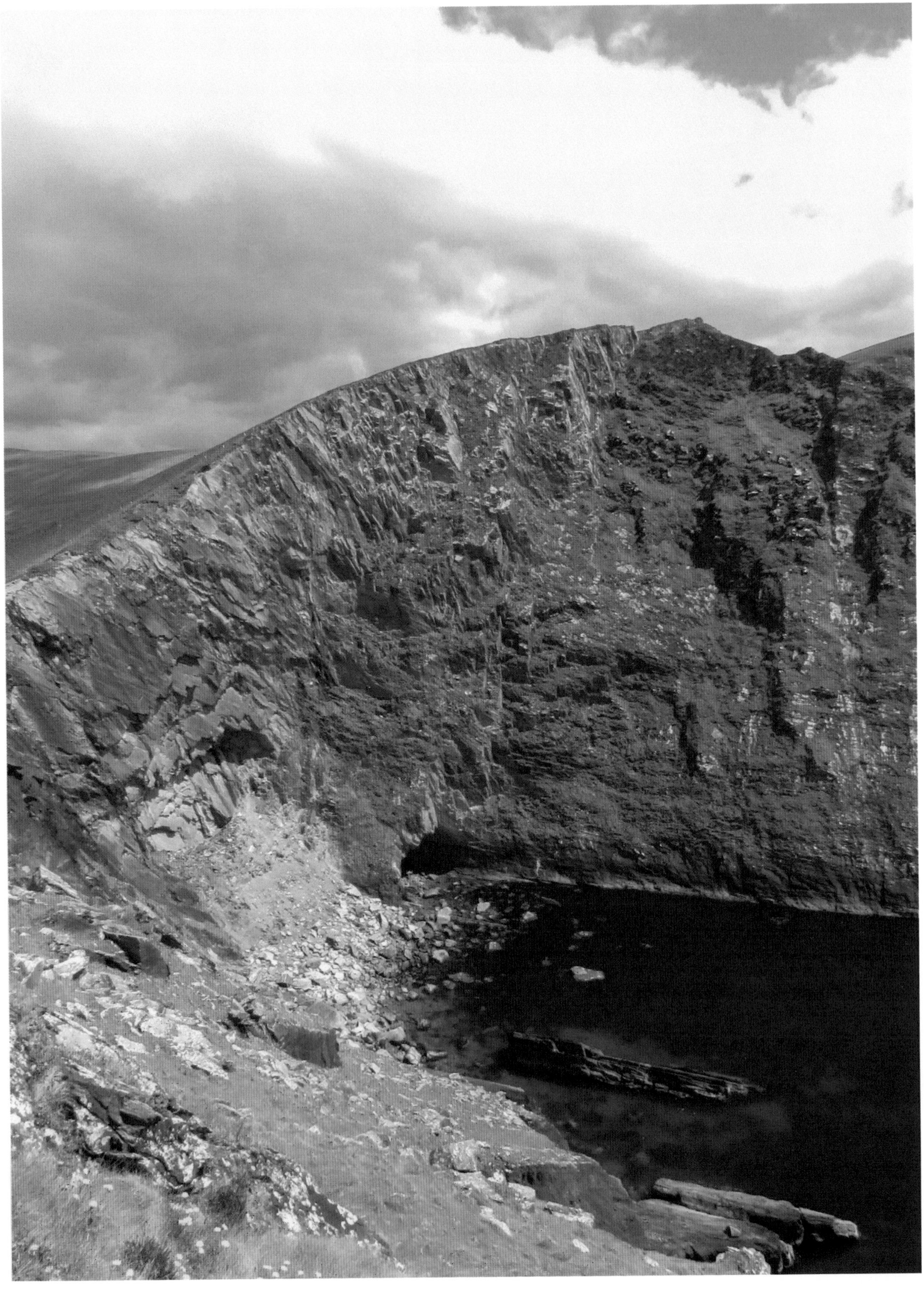

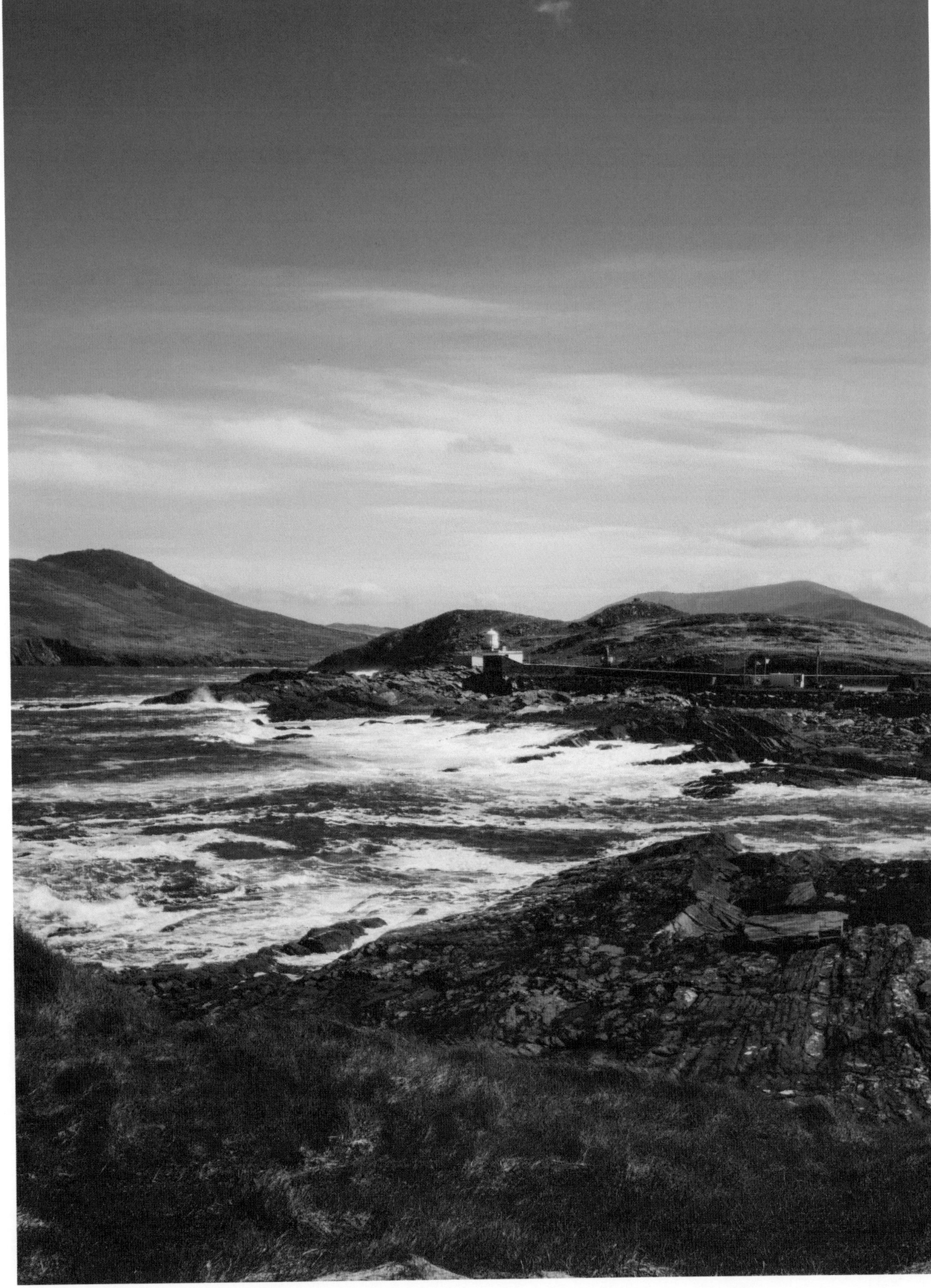

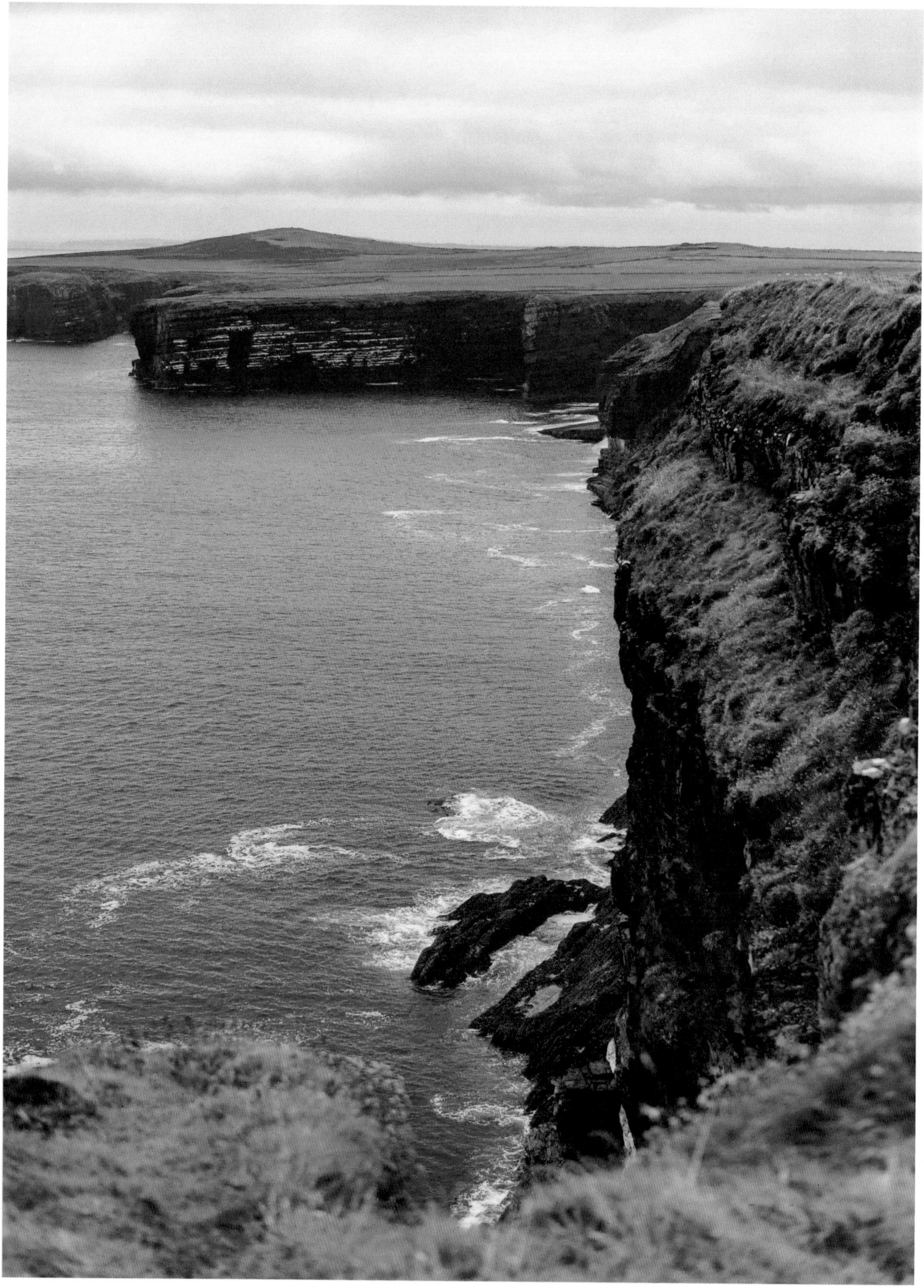

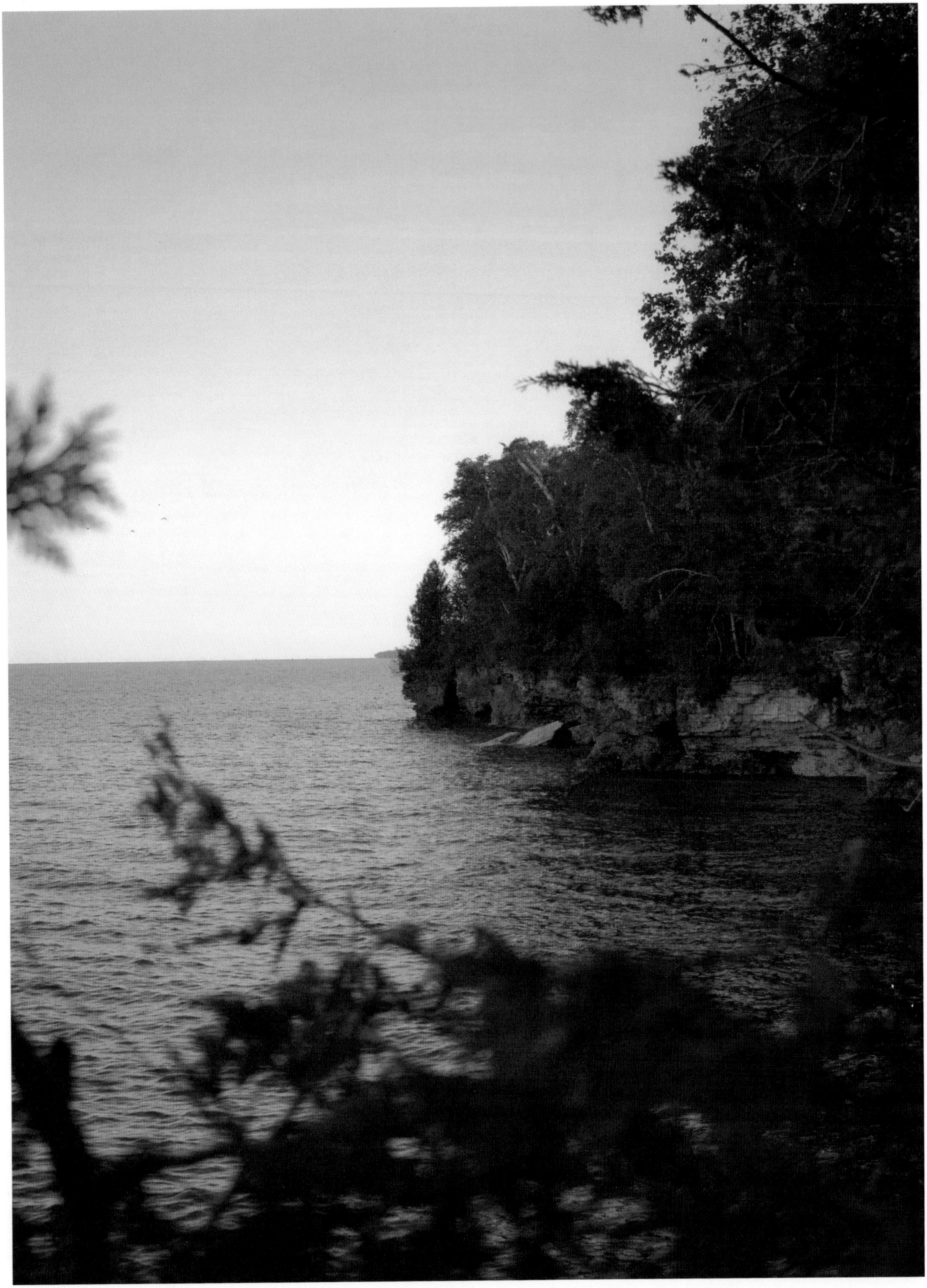

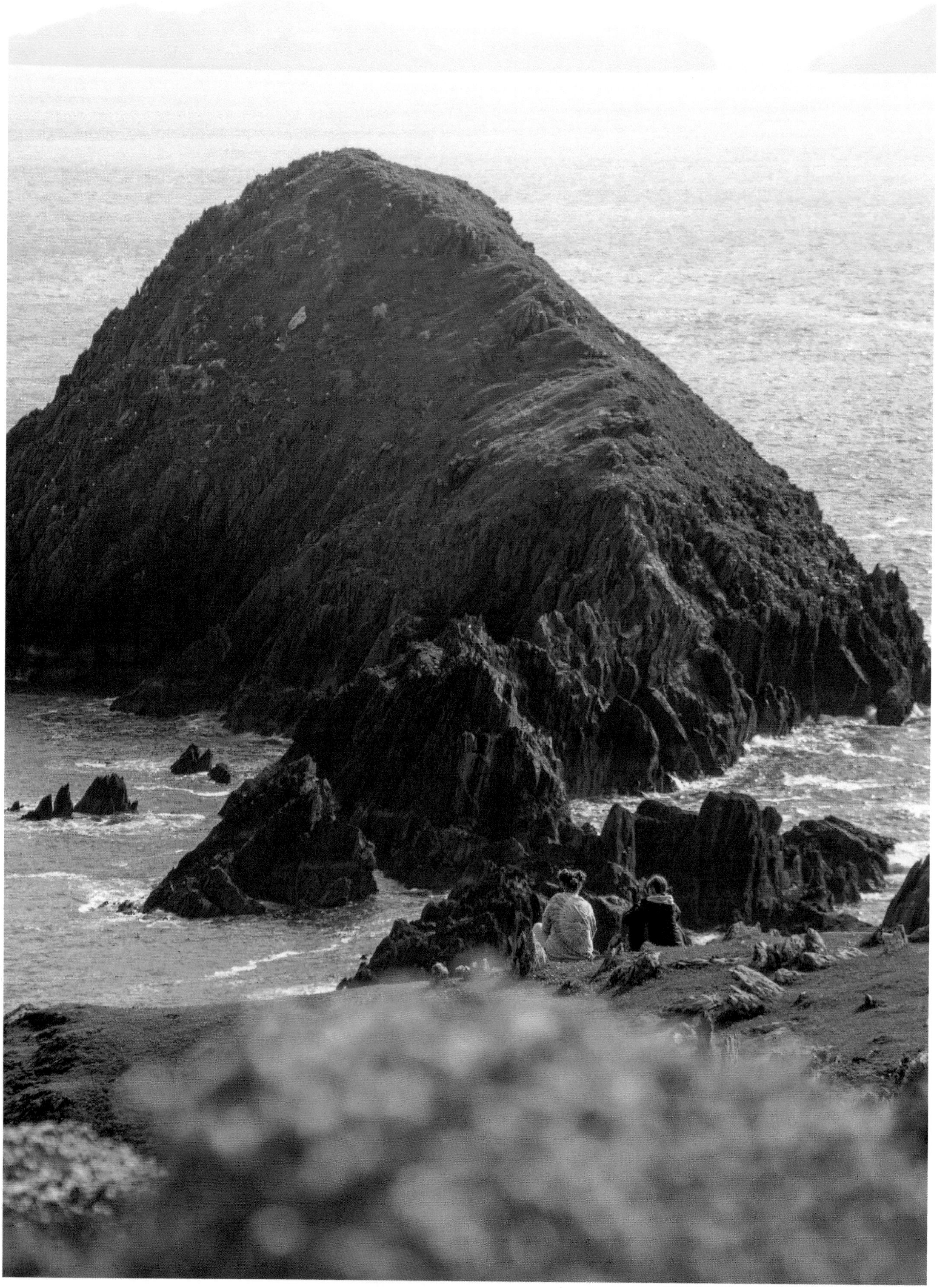

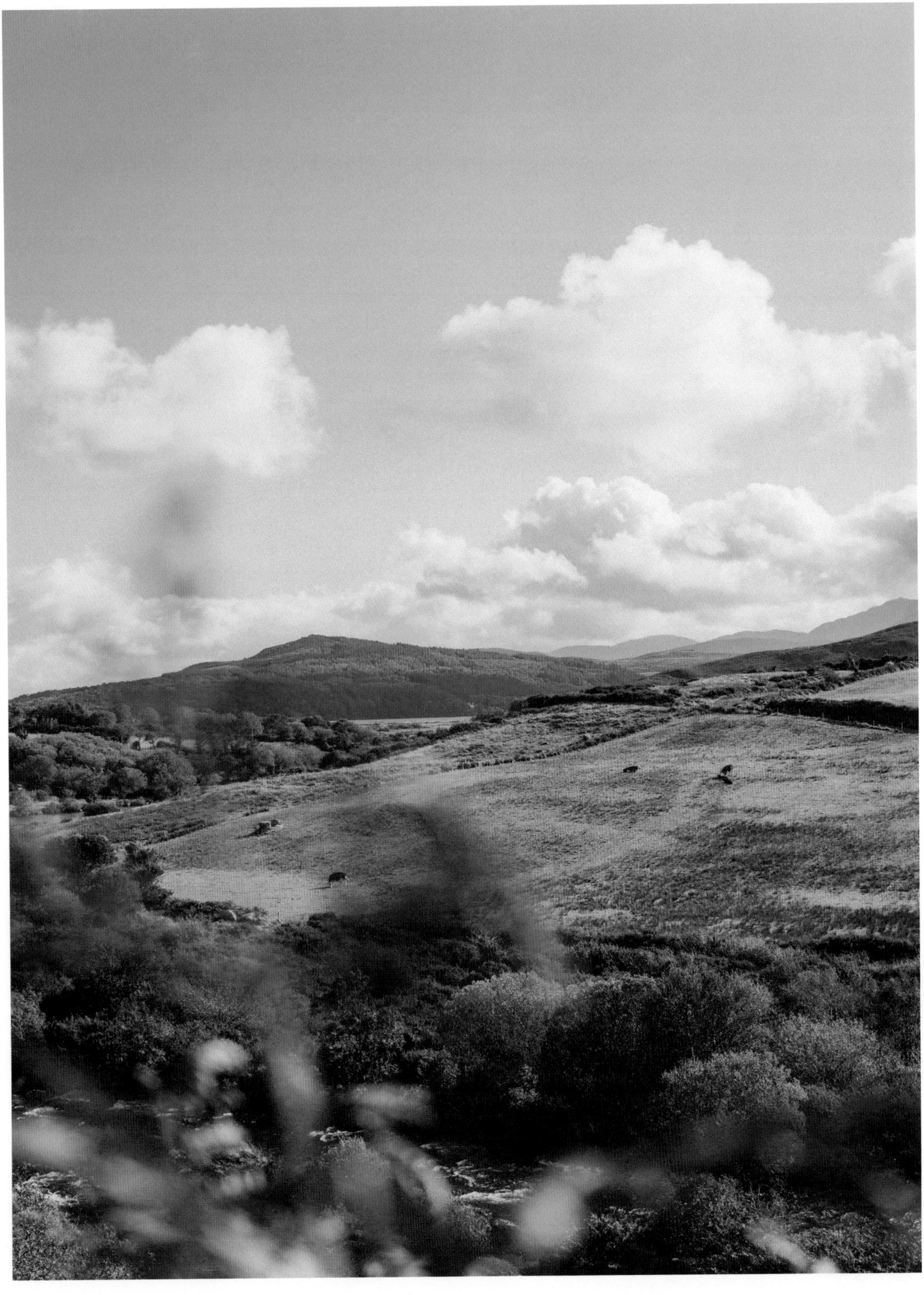

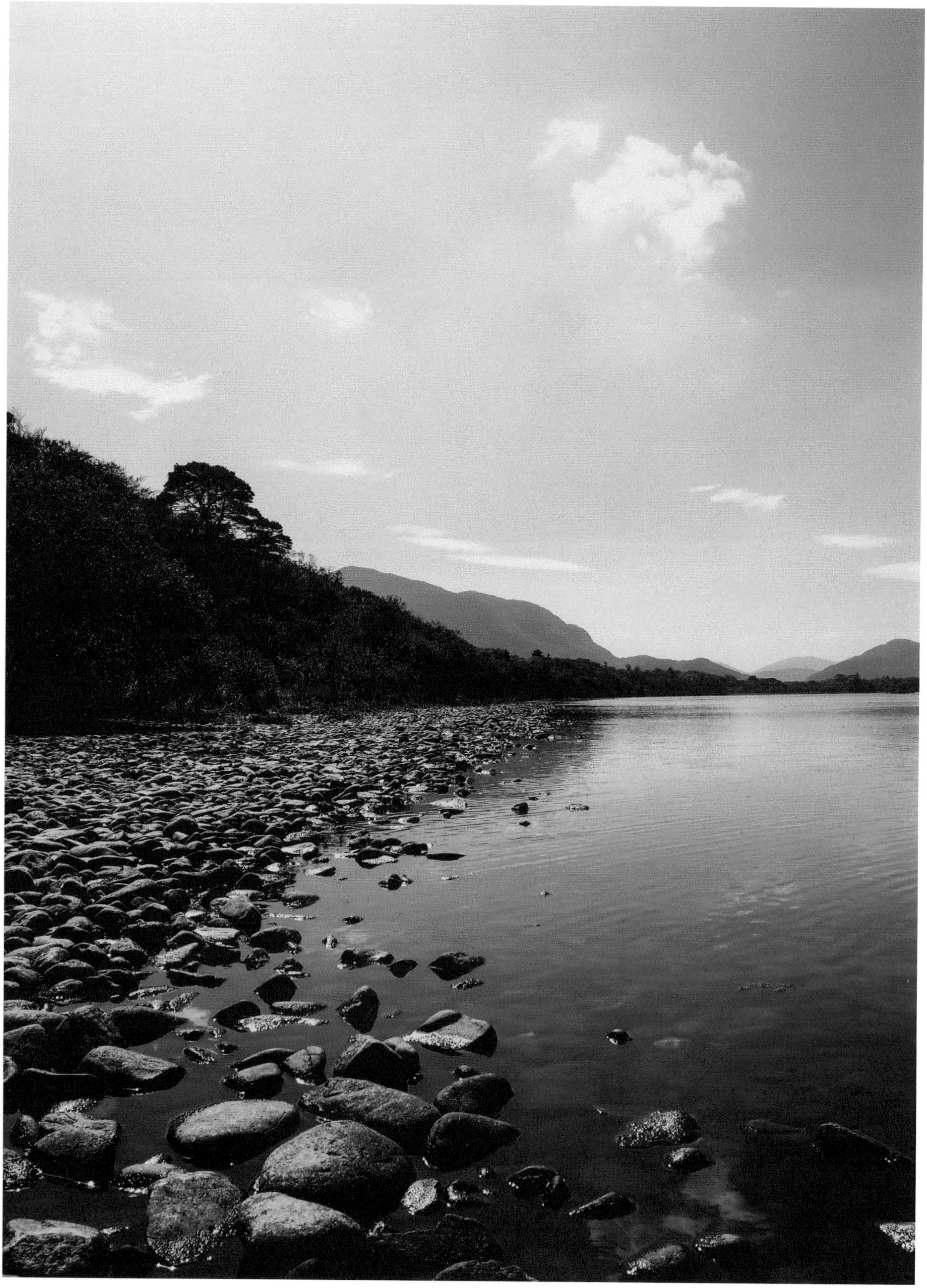

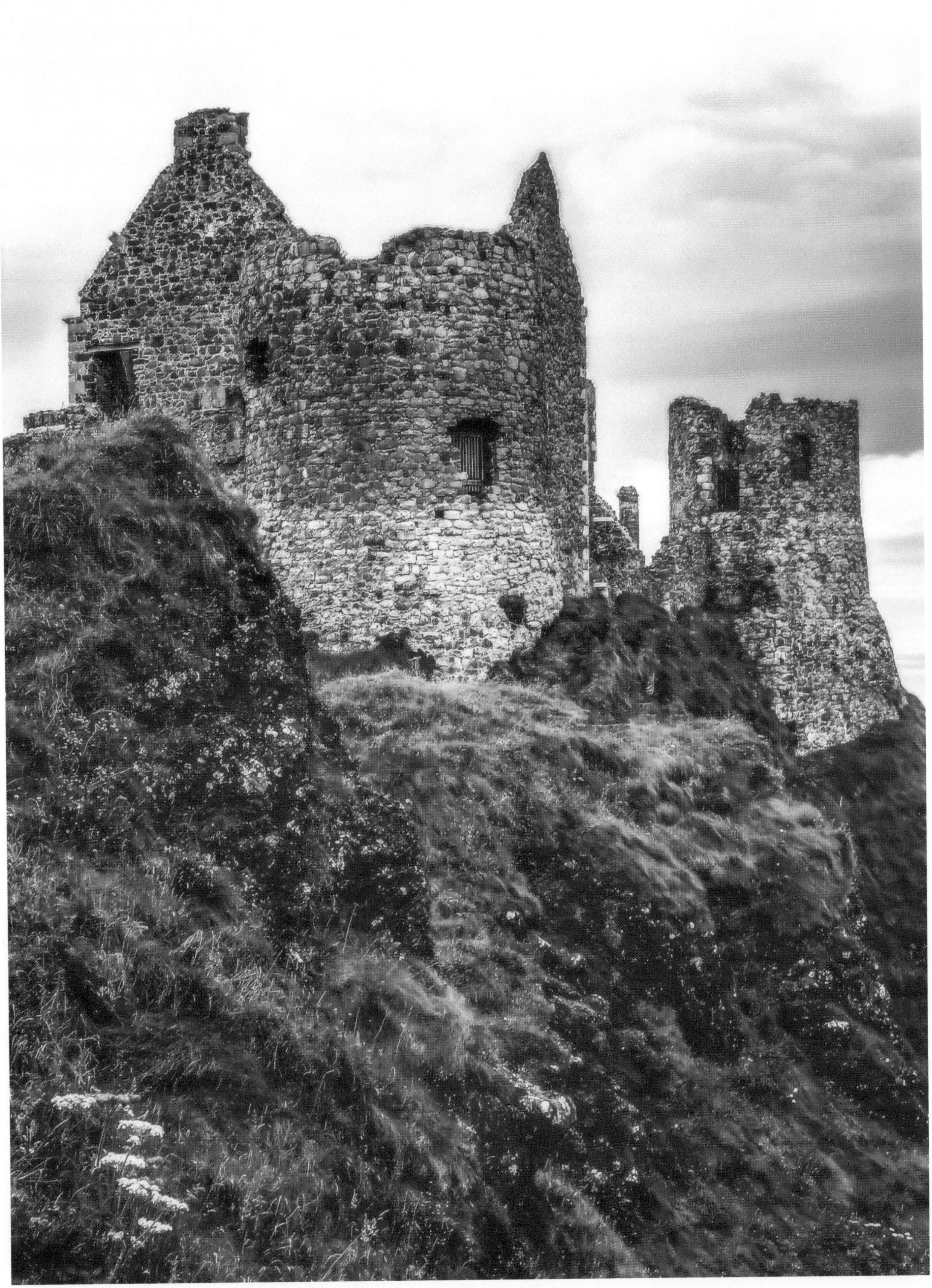

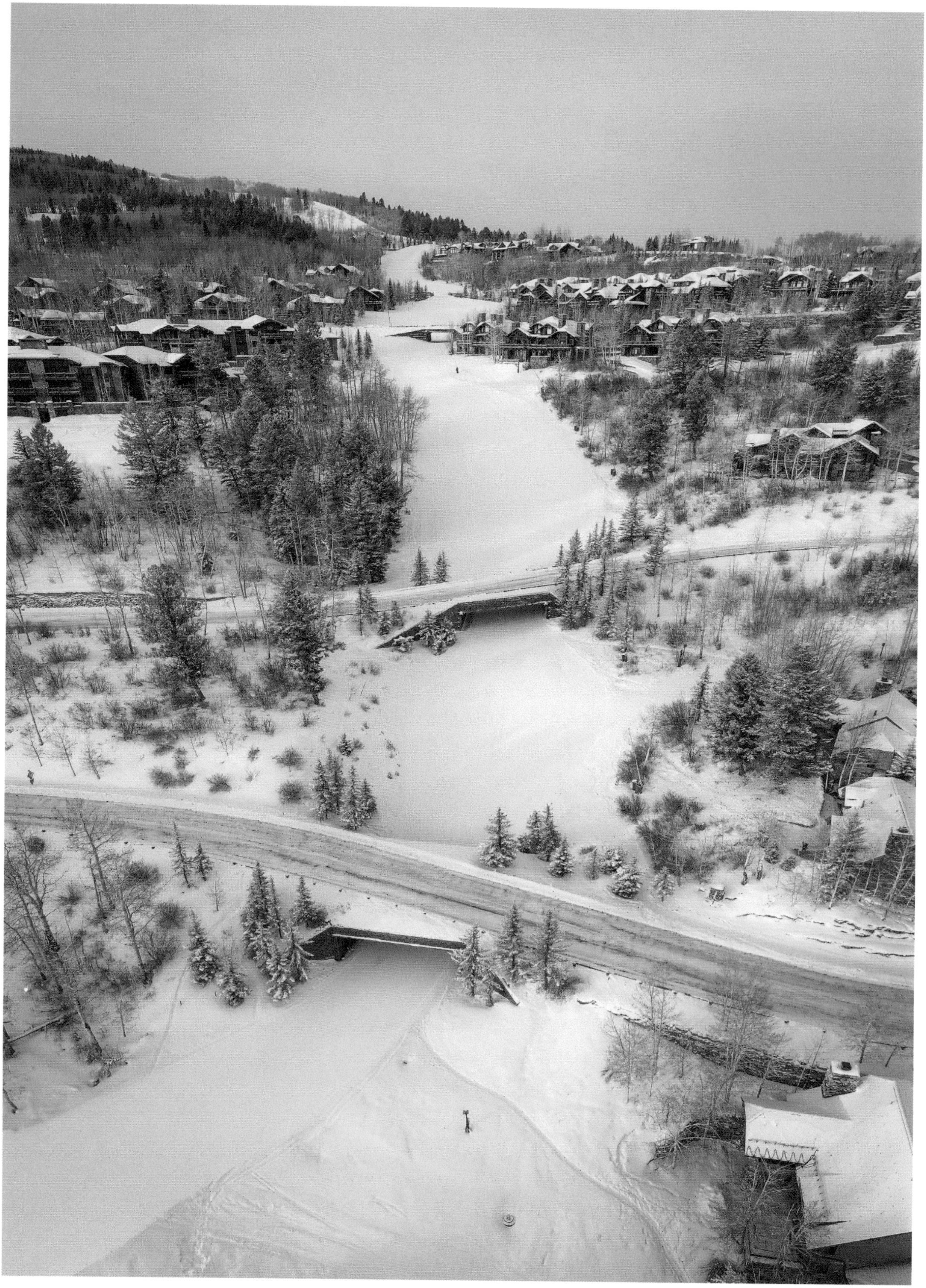

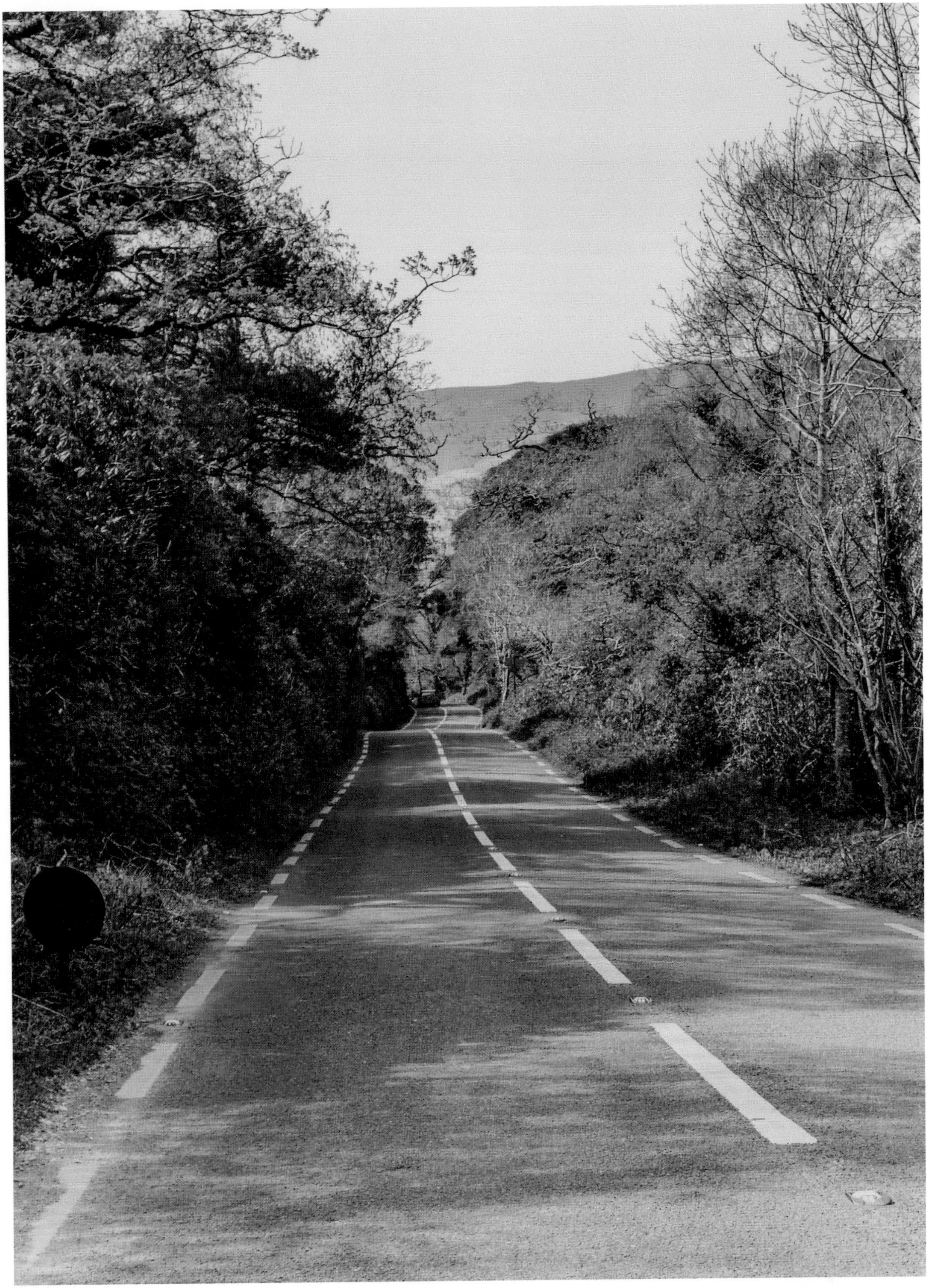

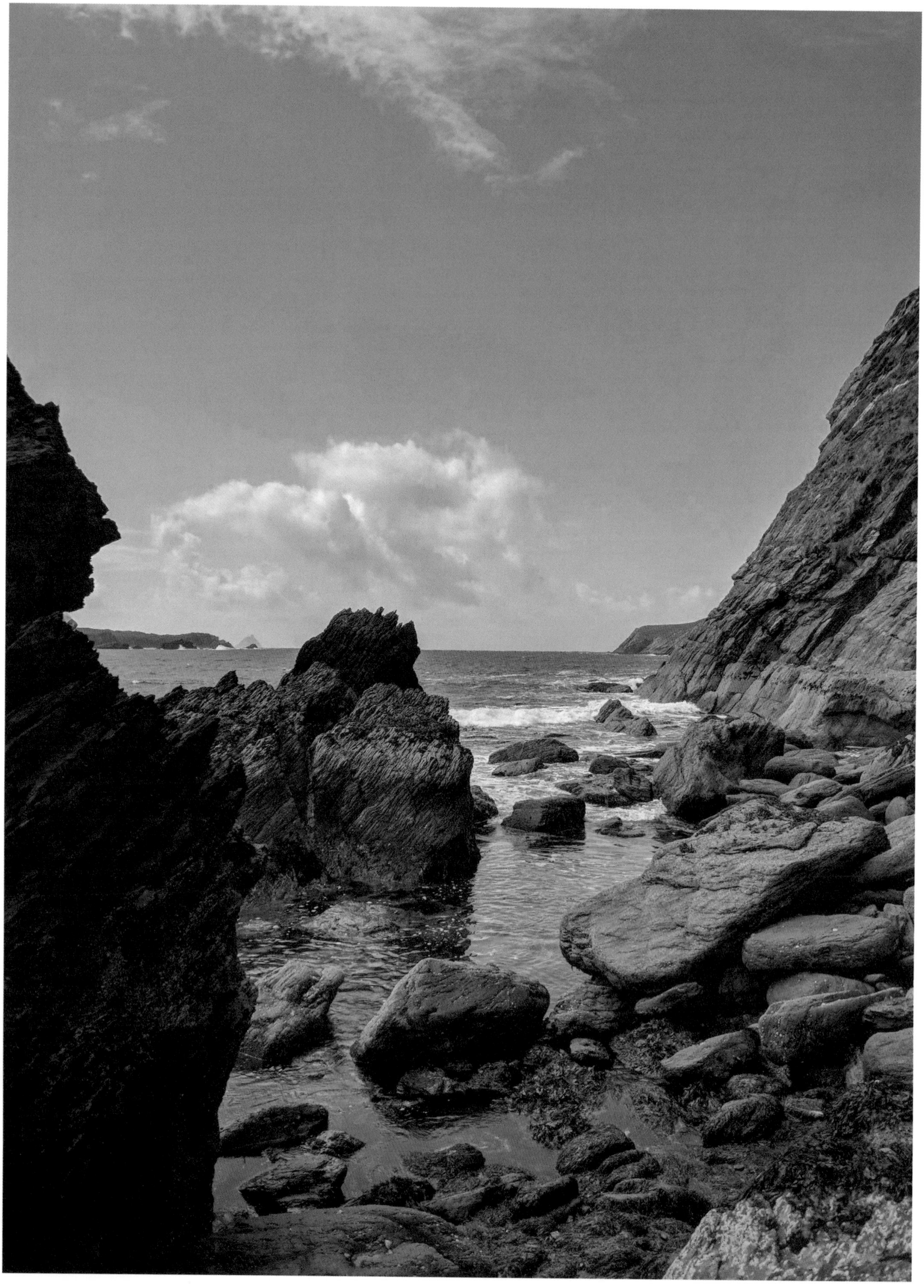

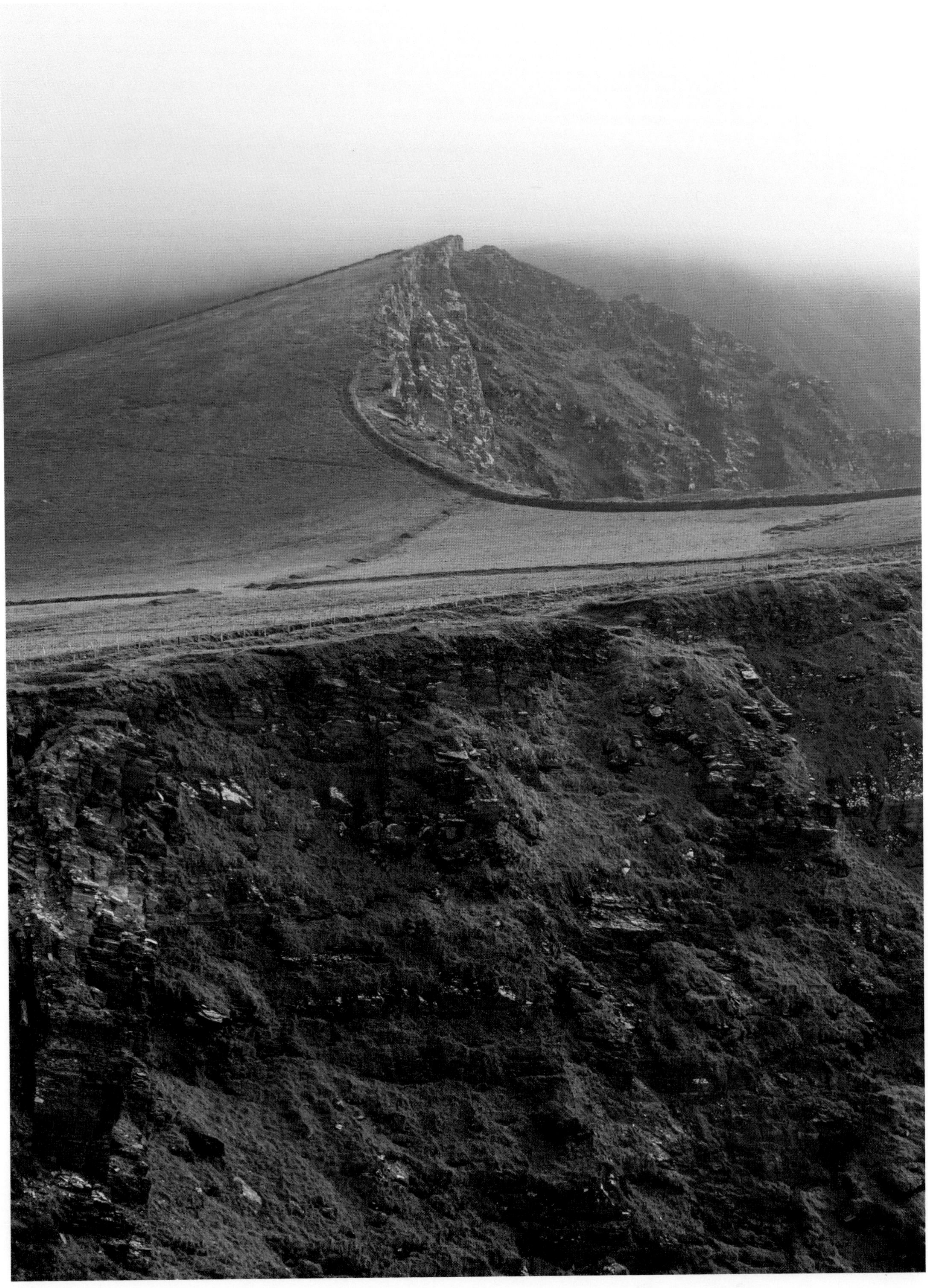

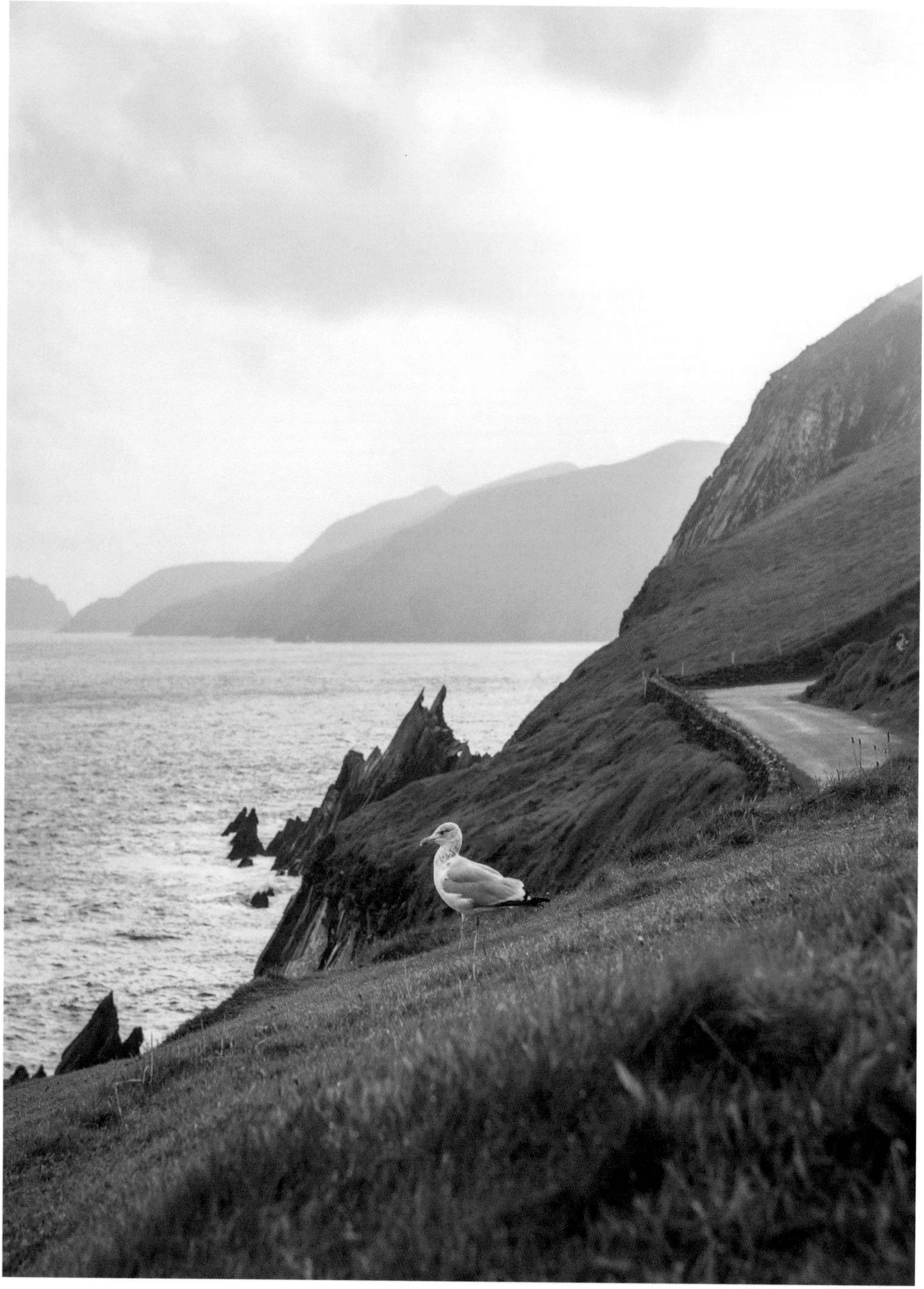

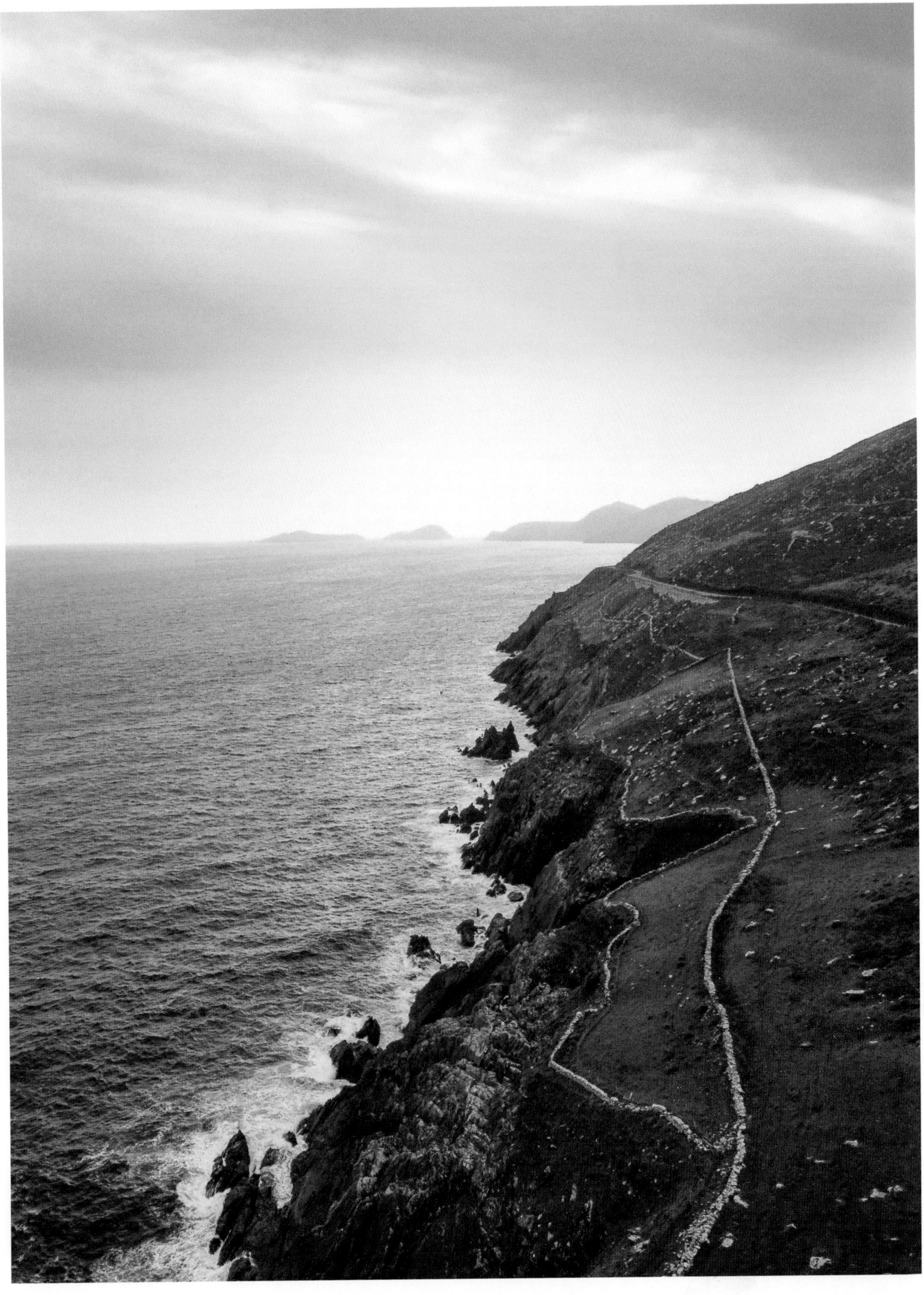

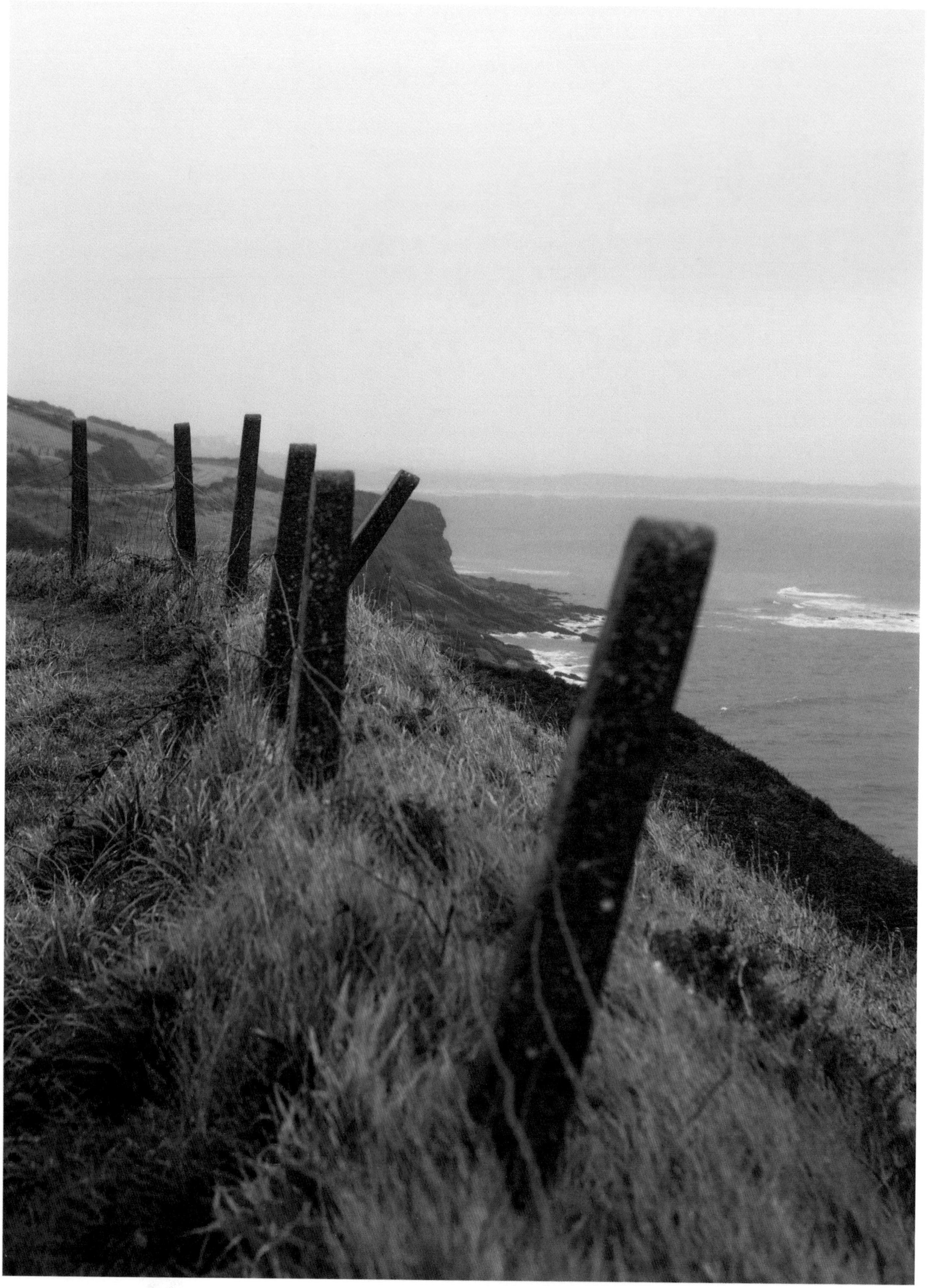

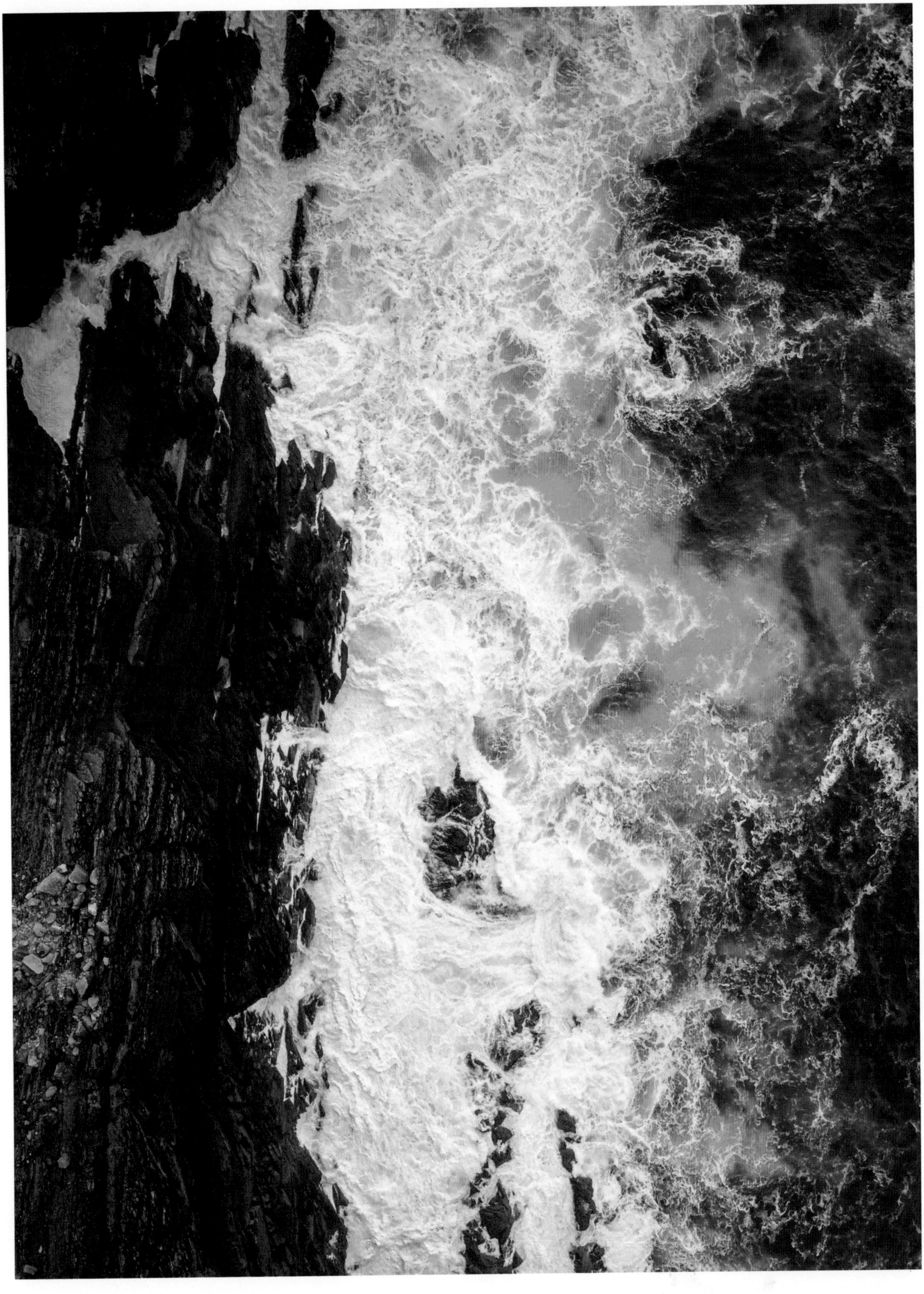

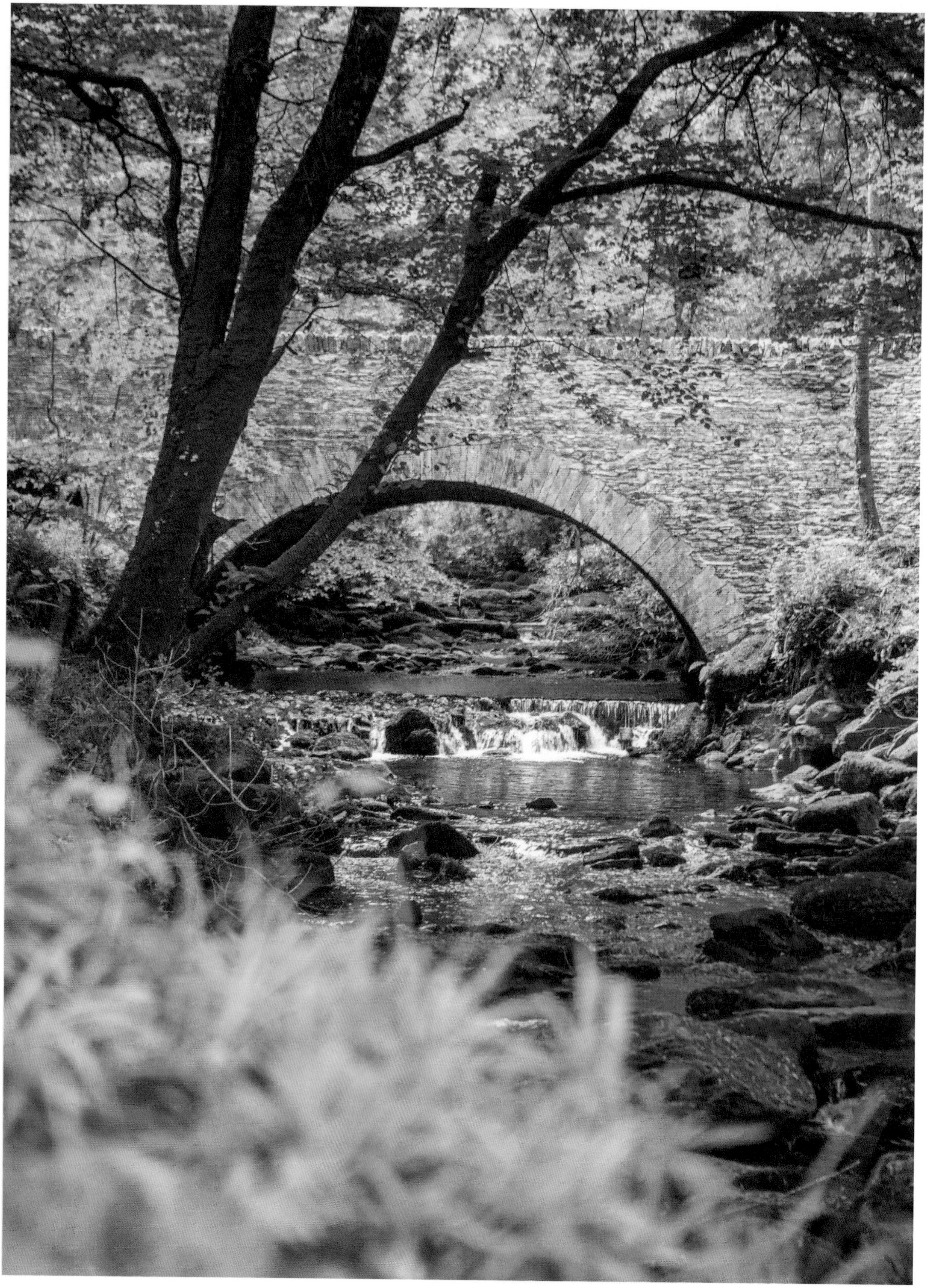

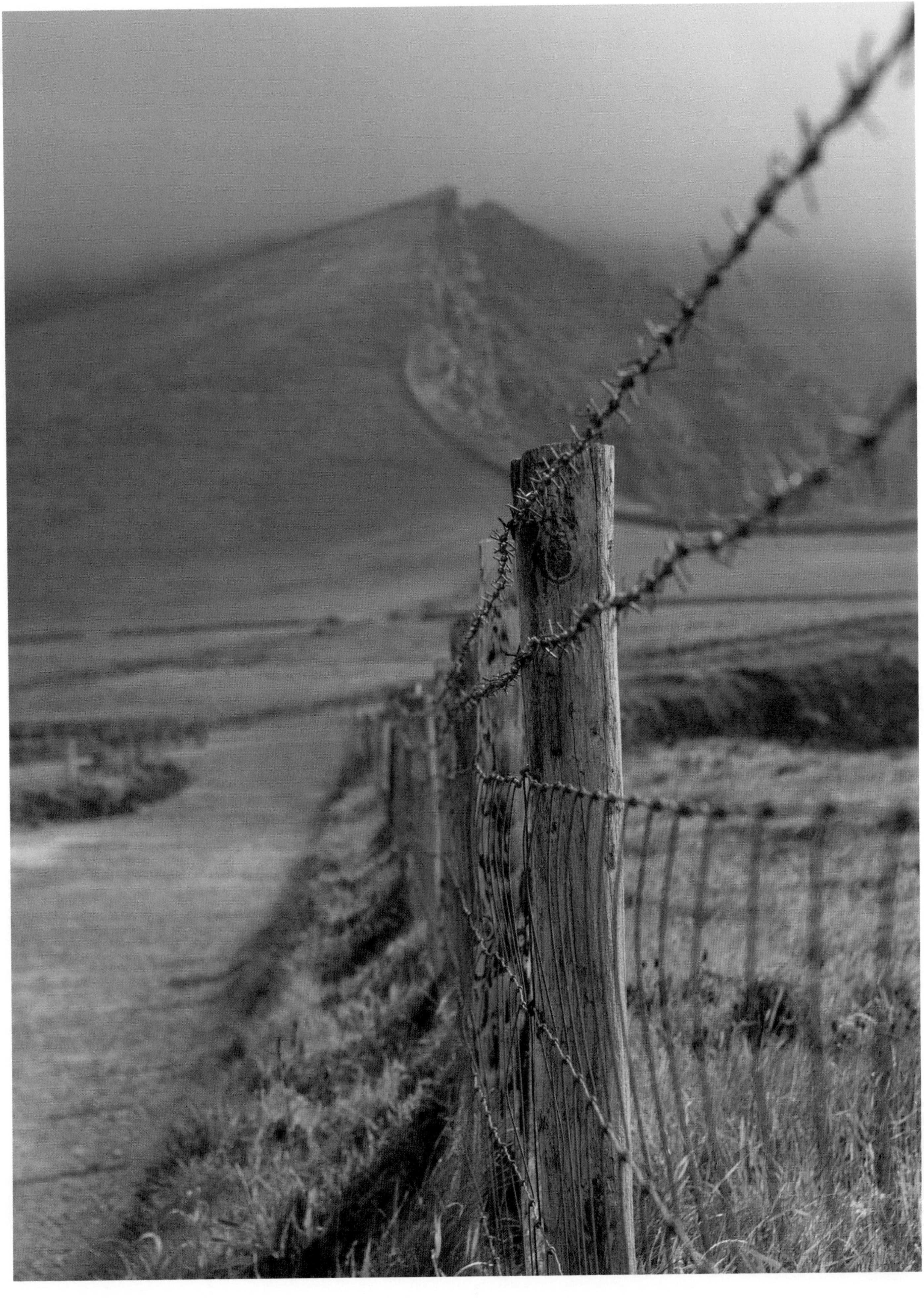

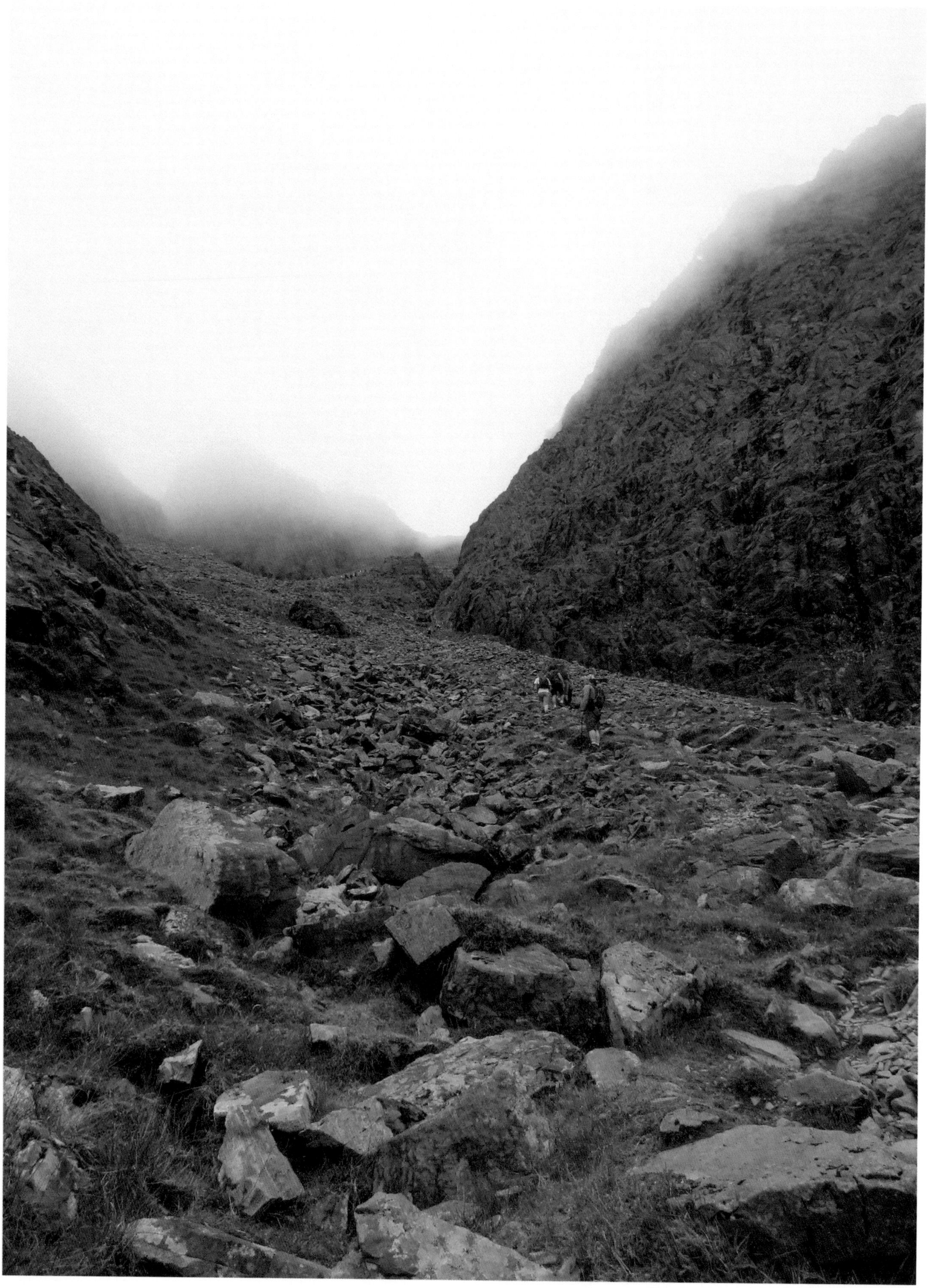

Printed in Great Britain
by Amazon

35030350R00025